Gestures of Orbicular Topology: Cheon Pyo Lee

Essays by

Sarah Hetherington
Arthur Menezes Brum

White Flag, Brooklyn, NY
Math Practice LLC, Brooklyn, NY

Cheon Pyo Lee

Cheon Pyo Lee's art models the ability to cull understanding. His work usually entails research into a system about which he has heard, the development of familiarity with it, and the rehearsal of its eventual outcome. His art wrests to a different scale the notably unwieldy nature of the information he acquires, recalling Jack Burnham's description of the aesthetic of systems in his 1968 essay "System Esthetics": In evaluating systems the artist is a perspectivist considering goals, boundaries, structure, input, output, and related activity inside and outside the system....For systems, information, in whatever form conveyed, becomes a viable esthetic consideration.

Yet, Lee's artistic production fetishizes neither information nor systemization: his work prevents one from ever imagining that the meta-position is a more stable perspective from which to apprehend the operations of the artwork. His practice asks us to toggle back and forth from the information presented in the work to the knowledge it produces about information acquisition itself.

Though what Lee produces often takes the form of sculpture, photography, signage, video and performance, or an intermediary between them, painting still harbors a significance bordering on poignant. Painting encodes the aesthetic of his compulsive autodidacticism. The act of painting itself tempts him to move "too fast," Lee has said, if pleasurably: in project after project, Lee disassembles information forms, whose audience's insatiable demand for turnover requires them to move "too fast" to make possible a practical understanding of the full complexity of consequential events.

By devising an object with the profile of a mass commodity but that is in fact a unique manifestation, Lee permits his imagination to turn mundane objects of modern life into sculpture: a cell phone, an egg, money. The research and development of the backstory narrates Lee's own literal curiosity about how things happen. The object or project models the concrete localization of abstract, globalized functions (such as money laundering in international trade) and the life and development of products and their wide-reaching effects in the macro- and microcosm. Hans Haacke offers a way of understanding Lee's objects in discussion of his own work: "A 'sculpture' that physically reacts to its environment is no longer to be regarded as an object [...] It...is better understood as a 'system' of interdependent processes...[that] evolve without the viewer's empathy. He becomes a witness. A system is not imagined, it is real." For example, he simulates mass-product development by designing a better cell phone, engaging a manufacturer to build it, and thereby taking the first step toward competing in the global market himself while simultaneously showing the ease with which one might intervene in it. Or, in the wake of the avian flu epidemic in China, which caused price gouging in the rarified egg market, Lee noted that Chinese business interests were combining real and fake within the same package to slake the appetite of desperate consumers. So Lee fashioned his own eggs (from wood), along with unique packaging, and worked with genetic engineers to devise "better:" their imagined prototype egg included sausage and bacon within its shell. Similarly, Lee's activities with money emphasize its simultaneous metaphoricity and materiality: he burns fake money, gives it away, launders it, and—in what may seem a remarkable condensation—presents a photograph of a bespoke detergent box stranded in a Chinatown laundromat and branded "ATM."

While Lee works collaboratively and imagines an audience comprised of his peers, the coherence he seeks serves him first. In this way Lee doesn't oppose, but rather cuts across Viktor Misiano's notion of confidential community, wherein one declines the possibility of affecting a global situation in order to meaningfully transform a local one. Lee wants to understand how global situations affect him. Put differently, Lee questions the value of a single direction toward which the artist orients himself with regards to the local or global.

Sarah Hetherington

Cosmology: The Great Planned Obsolescence

Oppression happens everyday.

The oppressed are constricted into painful gestures. If not freed from their oppression, these gestures are repeated and become a frustrated pose. As this pose becomes increasingly habitual, it engenders a humiliating posture. If this posture cannot be corrected, it ossifies into an object of misfortune. When this object is intentionally produced, an Obsolete Commodity is fabricated.

Money is God's body

God is often called an intelligent designer. Commodities are designed to exist, and be used in a particular way. This is their destiny. Currently, many things are designed to fail and exist to be consumed. Each designed failure's destiny is discovered when it is consumed. Never the less, the designed failure succeeds at being consumed and a new commodity must be designed to replace it. Each time a commodity is consumed, money is produced and exchanged. This is the profit made from designed failures and the goal of their design. Thus, money being both a commodity and a force that transcends material, sits as the ideal body of its intelligent designer, the fetishized body of its designer, in front the ever-consuming fire of obsolete commodities.

By The Credit Clouds of Heavens

From the unending fire of consumption, money like smoke rises from the sacrificial alter of commodities in the form of data. Above us, money or as it is called in the heavenlies--Credit is computed and travels betwixt invisible clouds. In world of cloud-computing every thing is pure, ideal, and immortal. Here surrealism is the norm. The marvelous both mediates and ravages the everyday from its great heights.

How to Launder Money from God

Well, as in accident times, the great heroes had first to pass through the underworld; a place full of criminals, pirates, and monsters. This underworld is incrusted with routers and fibrous cables of which even light cannot escape. Wizards hold powerful sway over the domain. They govern by the technocratic oath, which is only superseded, by the power of Capital, the most high.

Heroes and Villains

Away from the everyday world, heroes and villains fight each other, through trickery and slight of hand. The struggle is exhausted by the unmasking of disguises and in unveiling conspiracies. Heroes bend the rules in the name Heaven and villains make Law by the Authority of hell-- the artillery of Vulcan! In the underworld, these battles rage as the most extreme tectonics. These tectonic wars are measured by the Geiger counters of the Media. The everyday person, who let us not forget is American, is mesmerized by the bleeps and the jumps of the needle. The will do nothing until wars erupt or until violence melts the ice caps. Good luck polar bears.

Where is Cheon?

Now, that this brief cosmology has been described, at who should we point our finger? Maybe the target is Cheon pyo Lee. Lee creates this vision of the universe with the pleasure of the Deist Clockmaker and with the sleeplessness of the photo-journalist. It is a world which he has set in motion through his para-journalistic drifts- both geographic and imaginary.

Cheon's brand of journalism is not concerned with truth. Truth is replaced with gestures and possibilities. These gestures are formal and topological, insinuating connections be what is and what could be. As a result, possibility overrides the necessity of facts. Lee is the universe's muck-raker, finding scams and corruption ad absurdum. In case there is nothing to report, he turns on the charm. Boredom requires charisma.

But, he is in no way above the underhanded world he has fabricated. Lee knows his livelihood resides in the commodities he markets. Thus, he does not intervene. Of course, this self-awareness has a cost.

Guilt. Maybe pain.

Asking again, who is to blame? The problem of the para-journalist is when one points a finger, there are always three pointing back. Everyone must laugh nervously. Our tactic agreements with the underworld create a sinisterly broad appeal.

Arthur Menezes Brum

Catalogue of Works

Texts accompanying the works in the catalogue
were written by Cheon Pyo Lee.

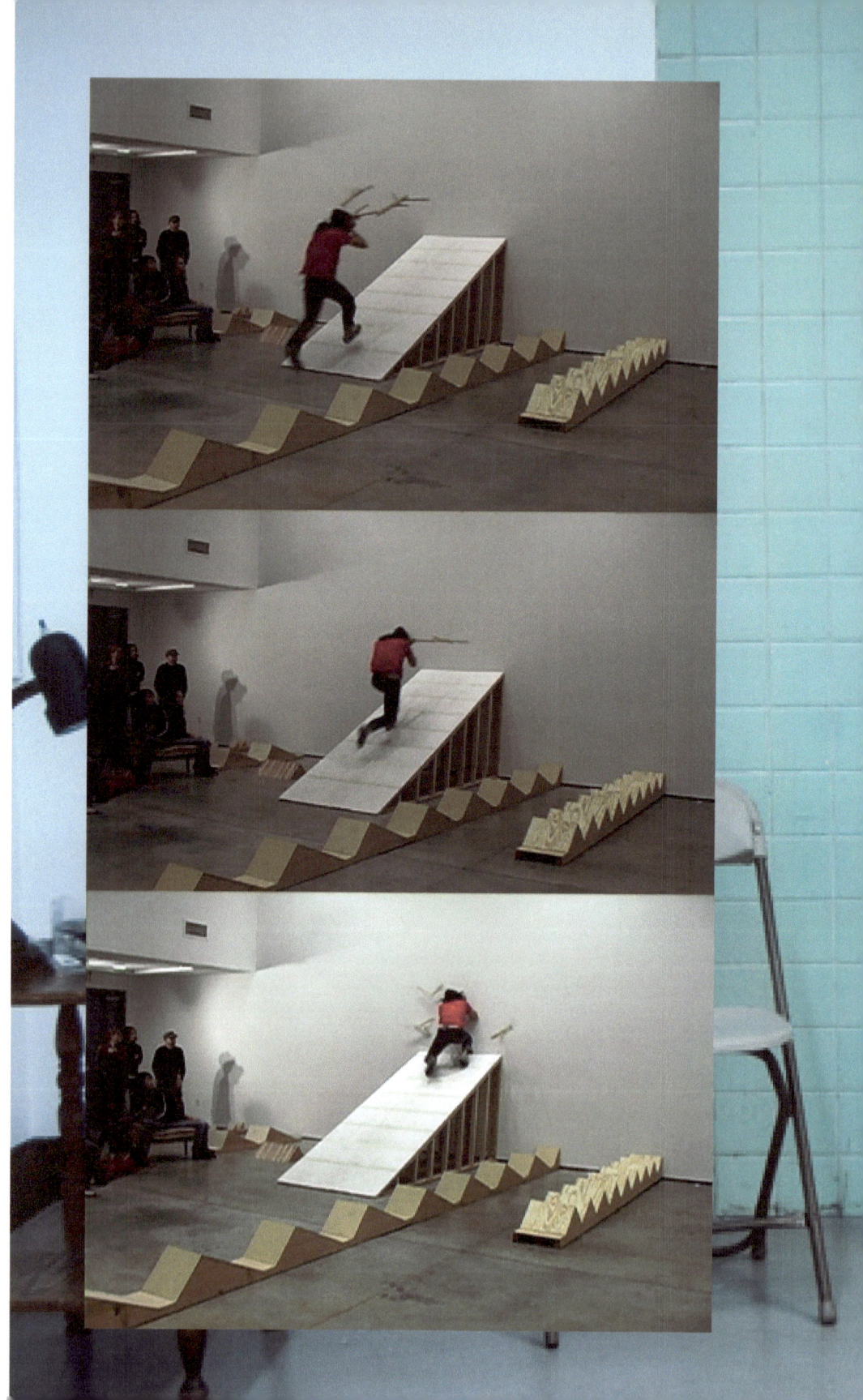

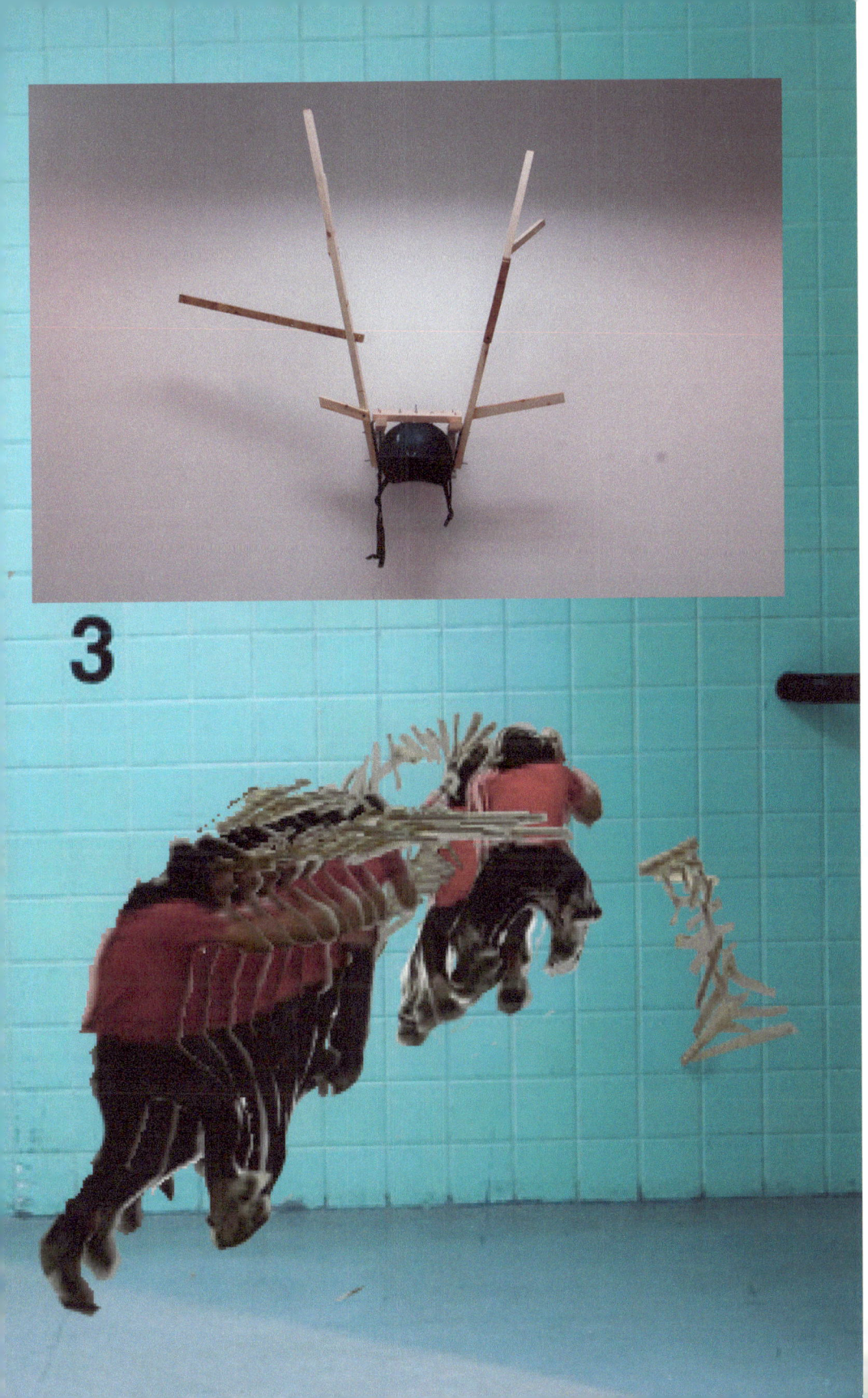

3

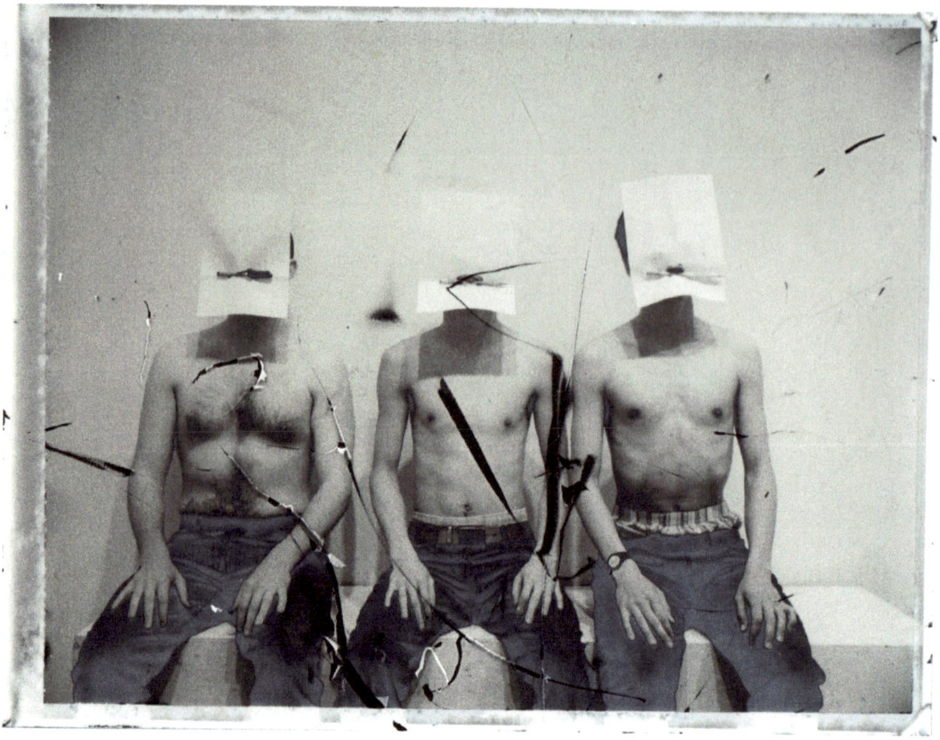

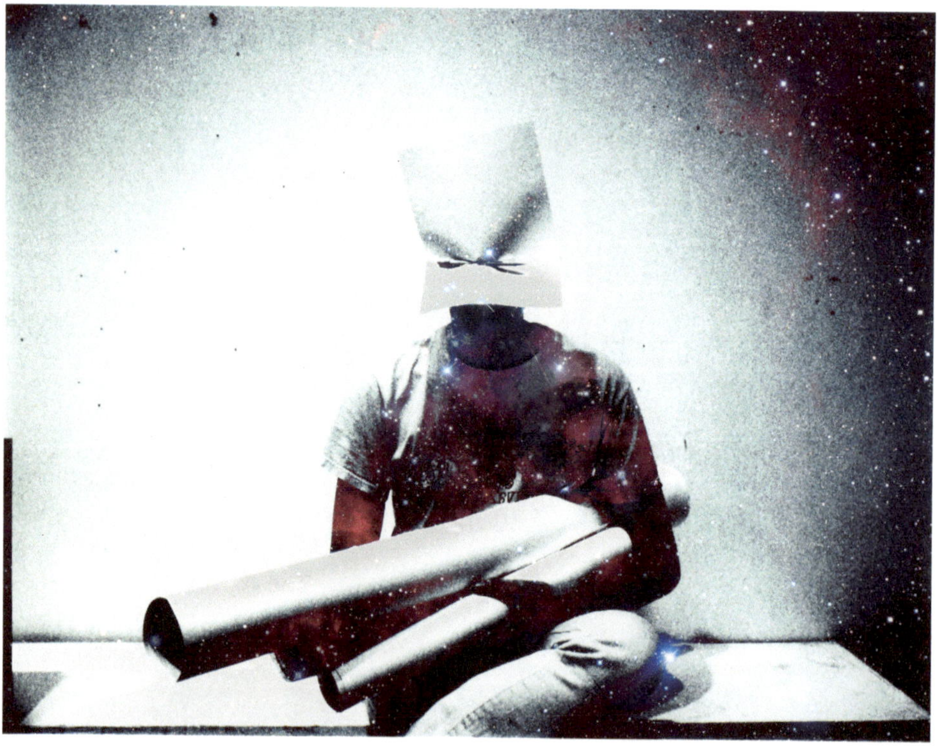

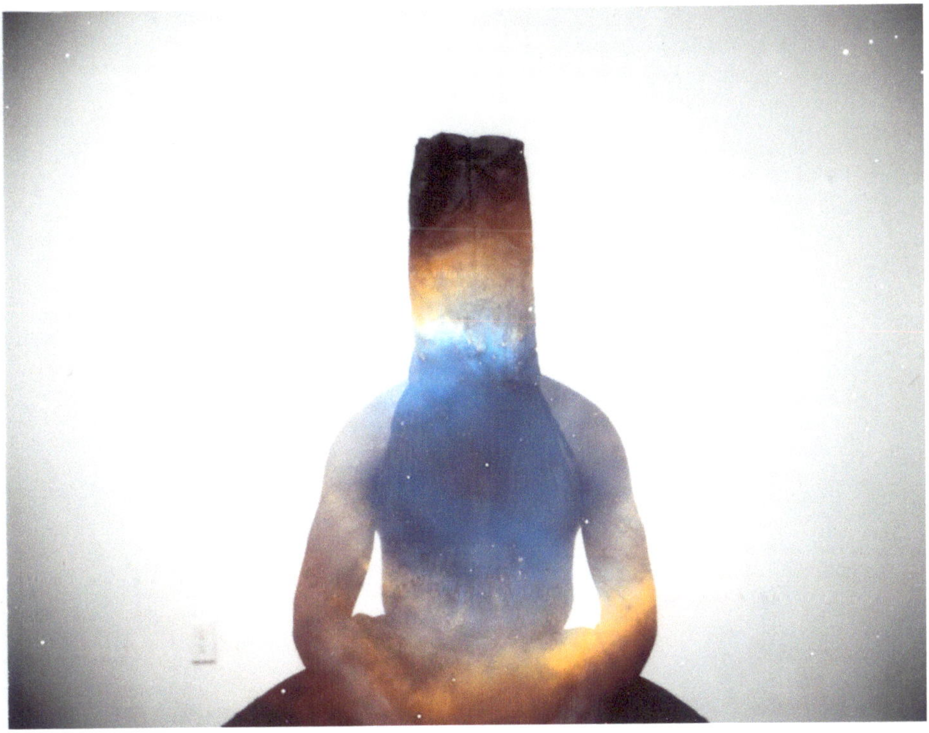

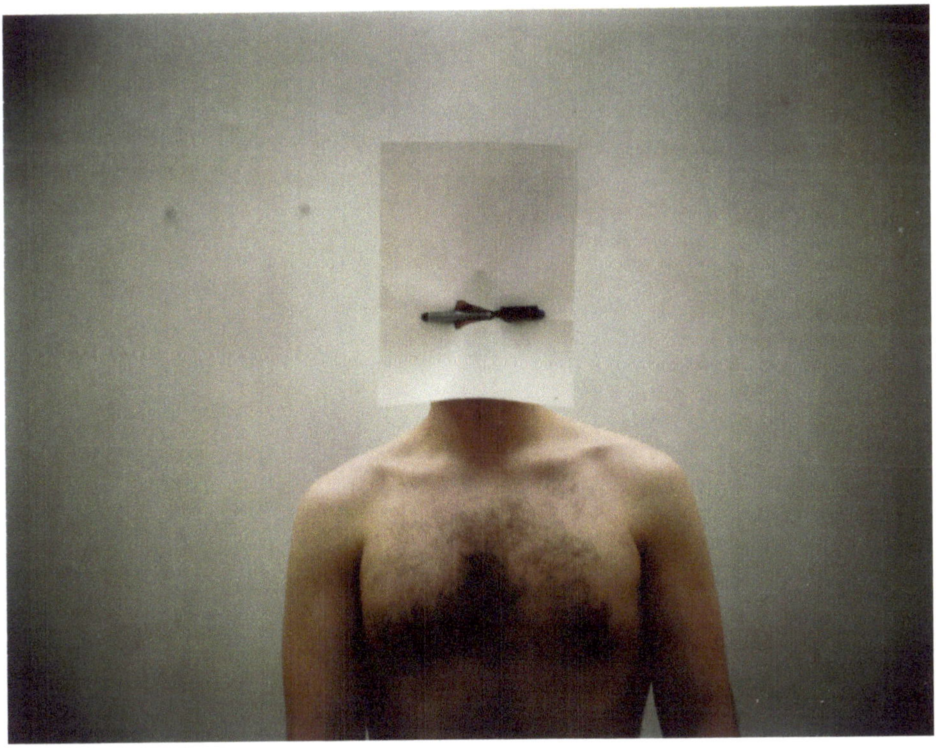

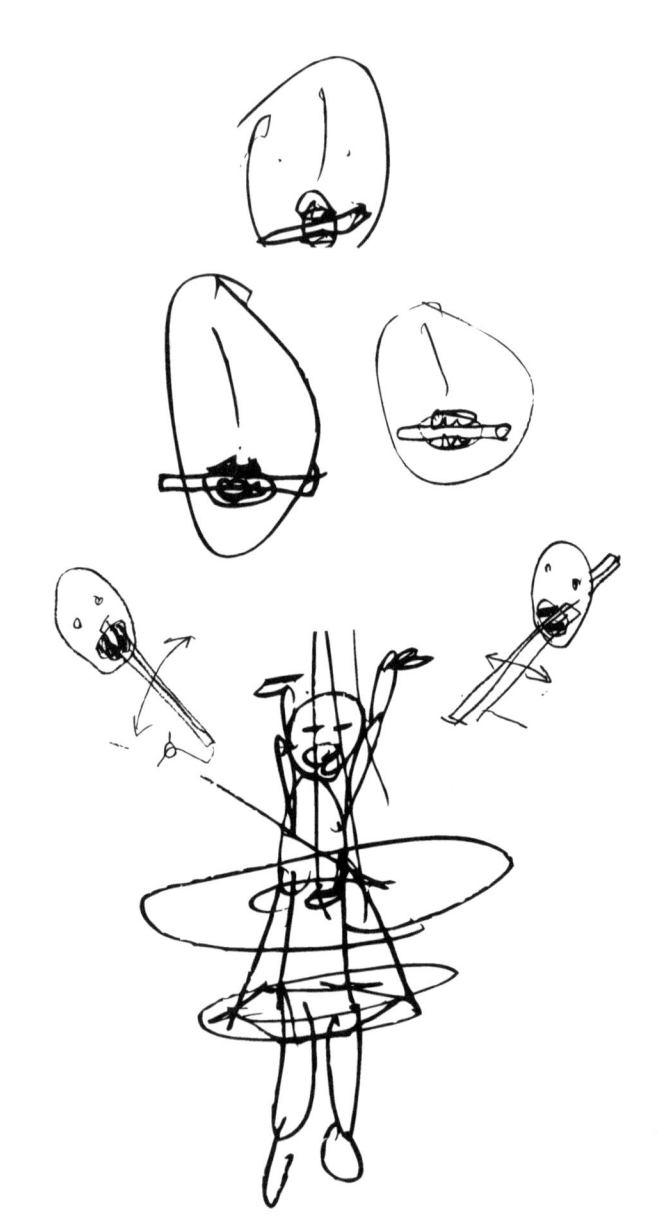

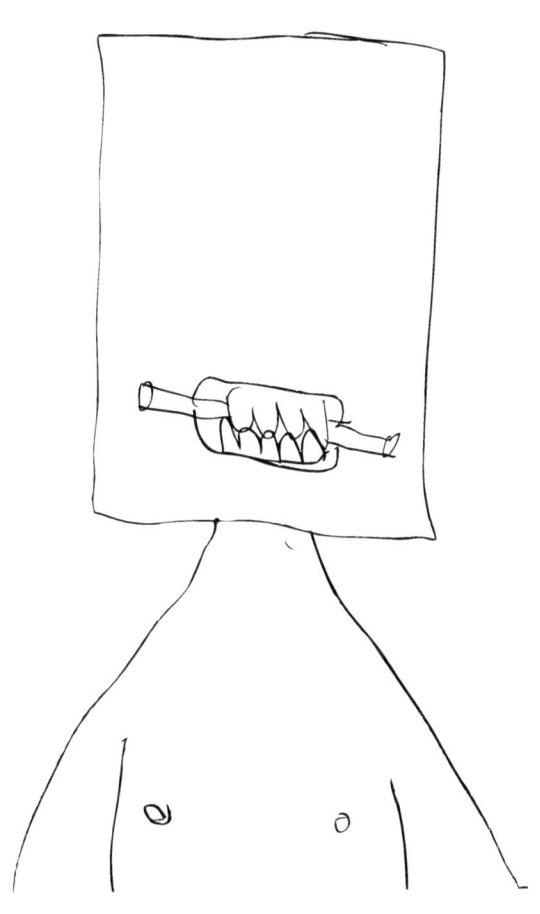

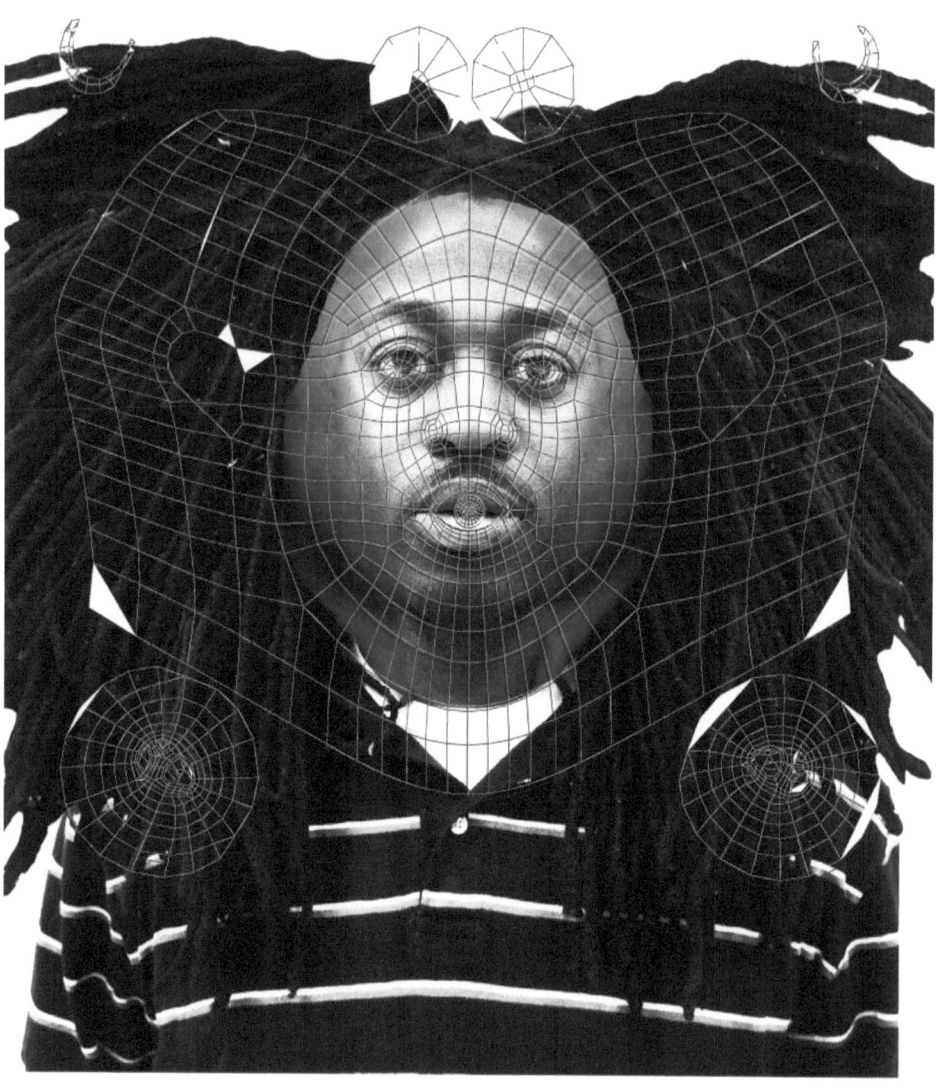

Body gesture are violent. It demands an immediate reaction that is beyond the signs of image. Because there are limits to text and images and narrative, instinctively we return to gestures.

Pain as meaning,
The landscape is out side, pain is inside.
The landscape is out side, pain is inside.

Pain produces gestures, and landscapes are built of gestures.
The source of the pain itself is not transferrable.

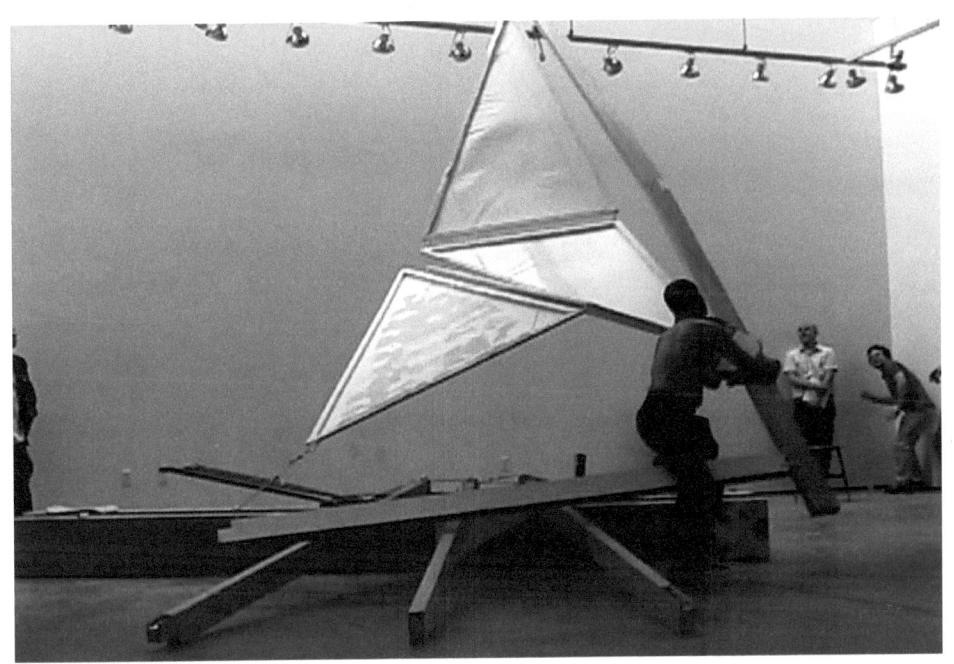

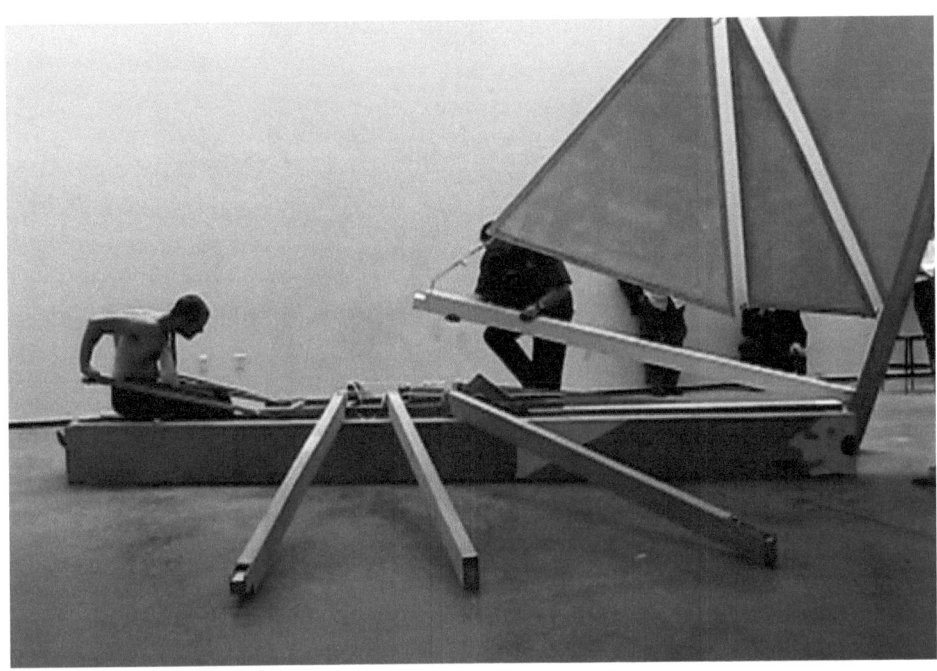

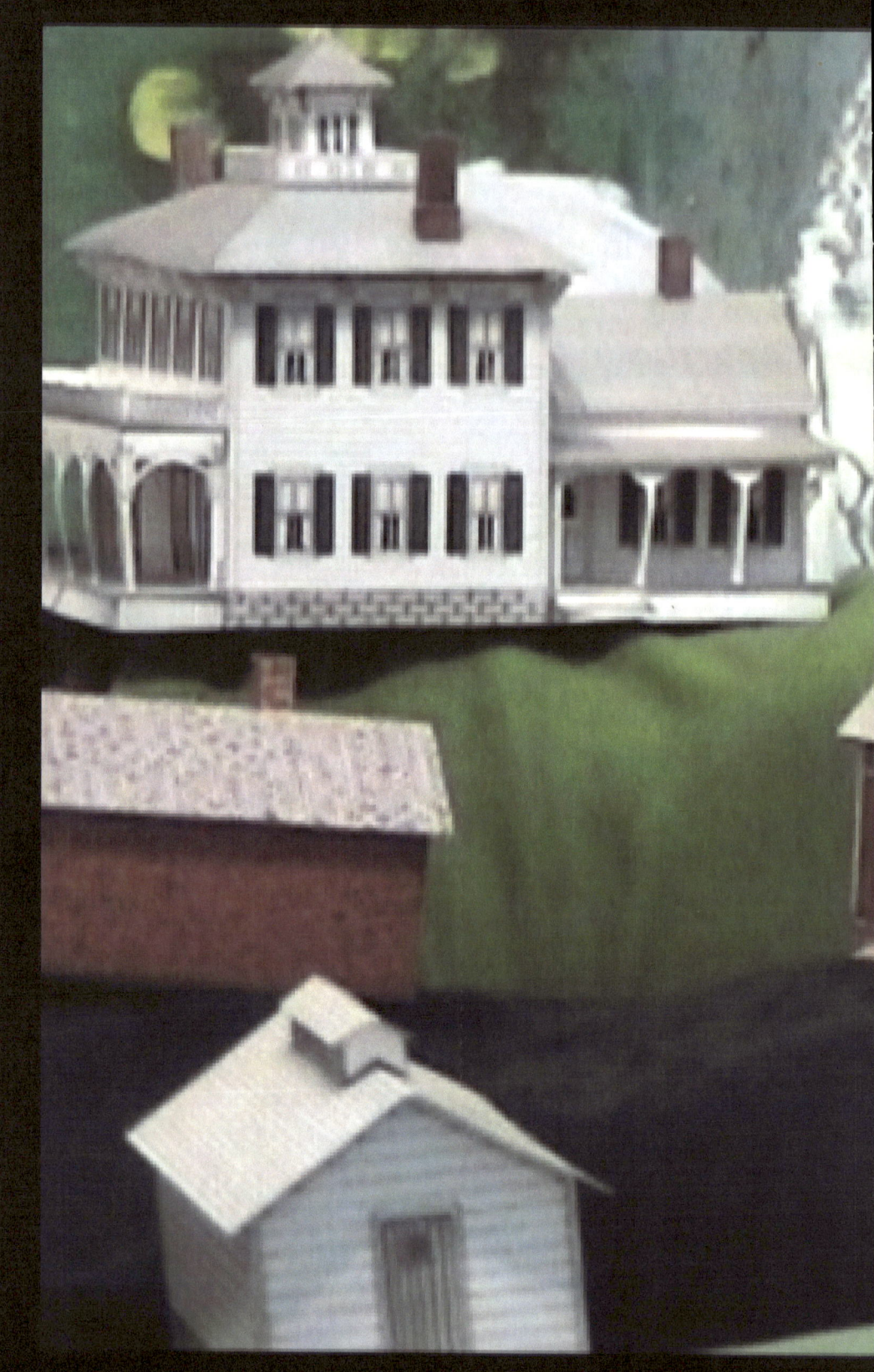

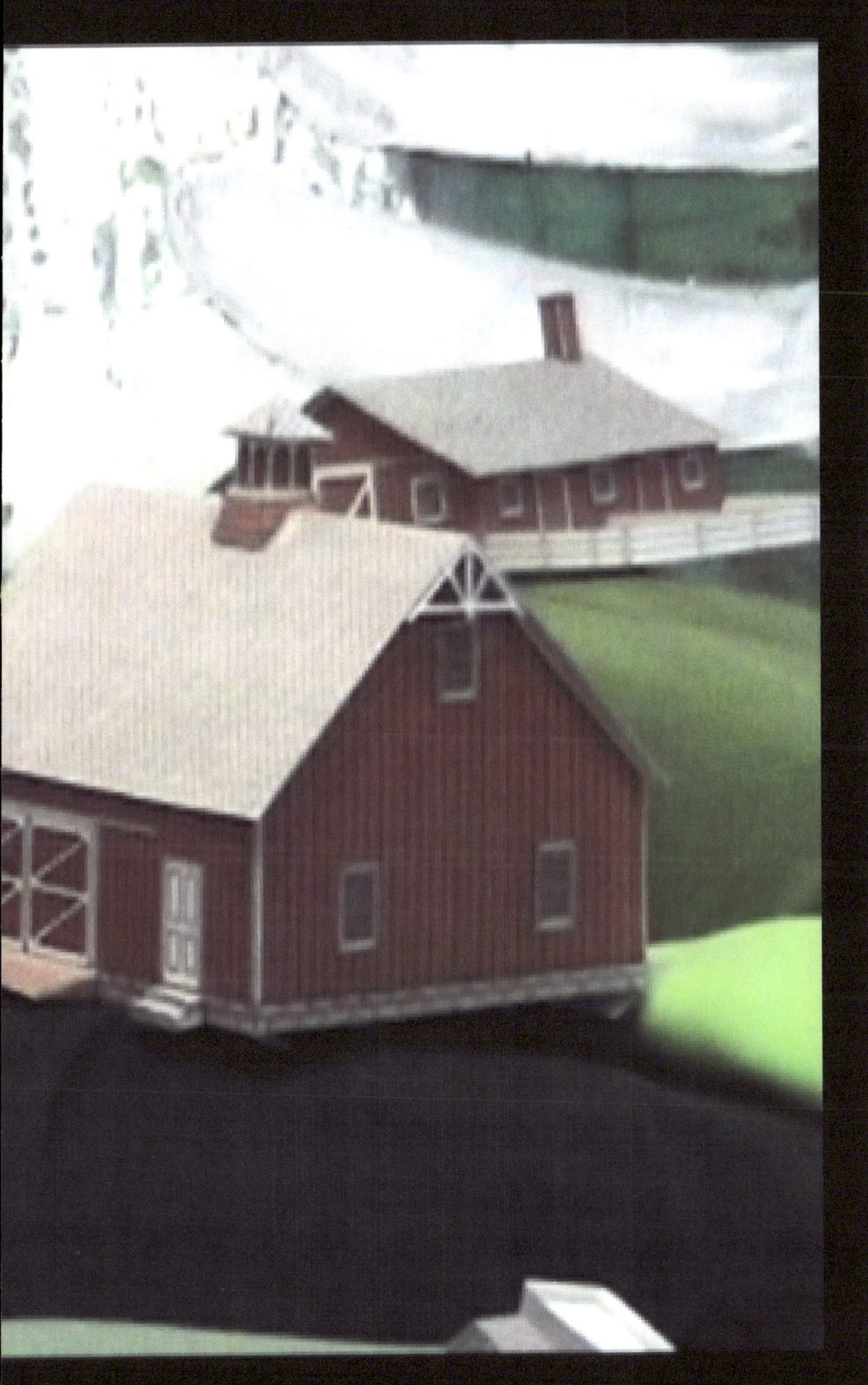

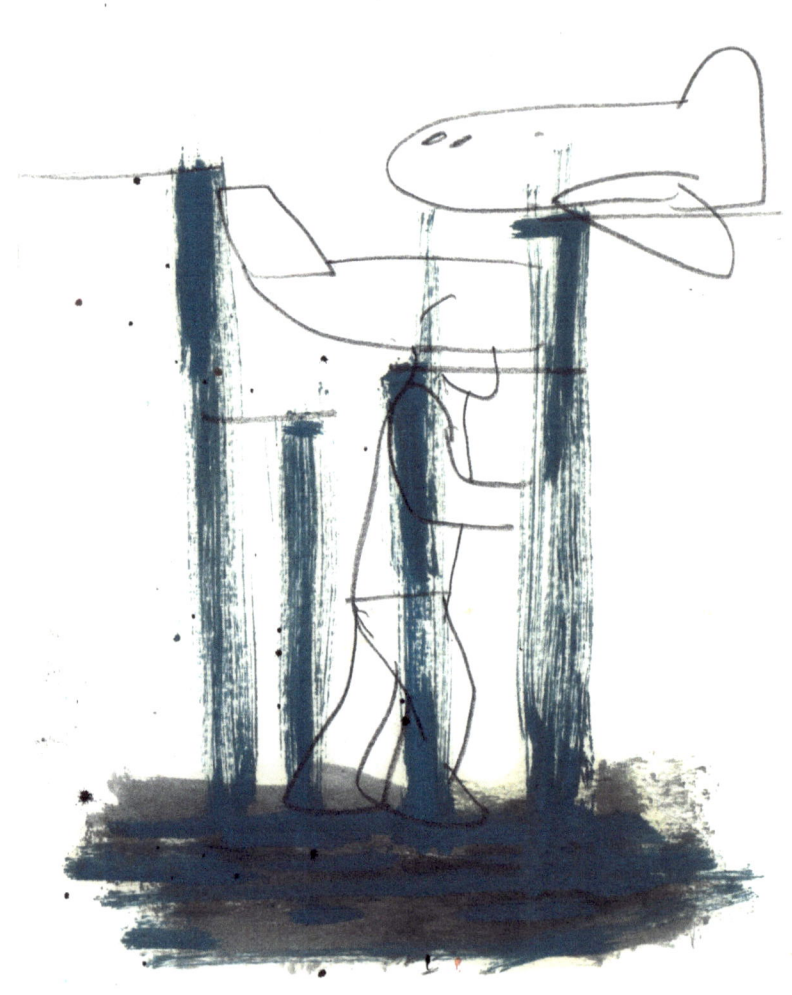

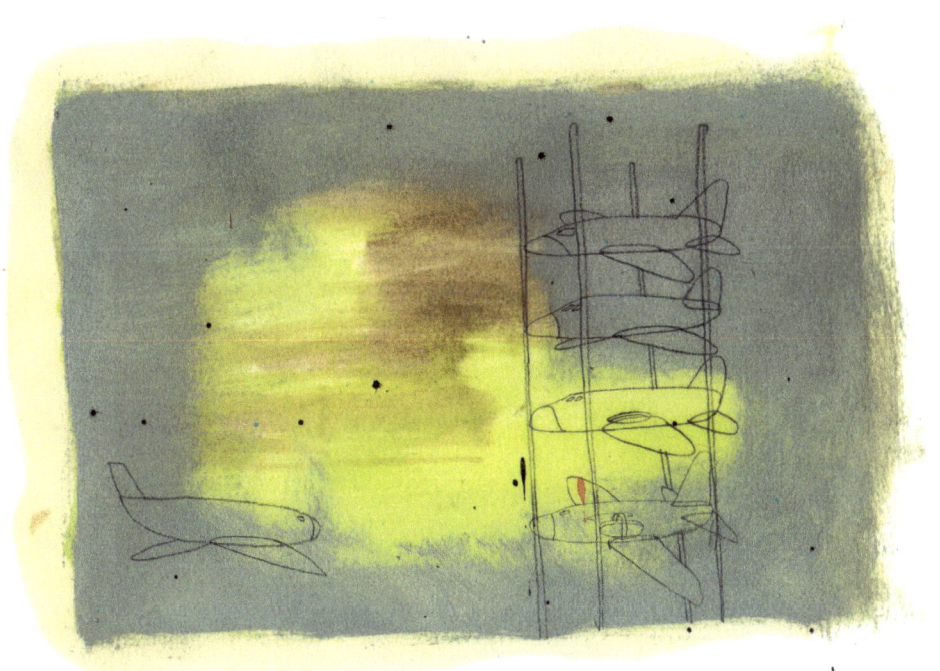

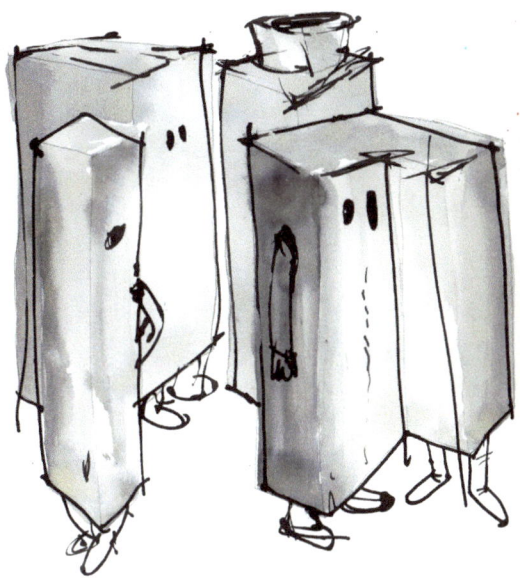

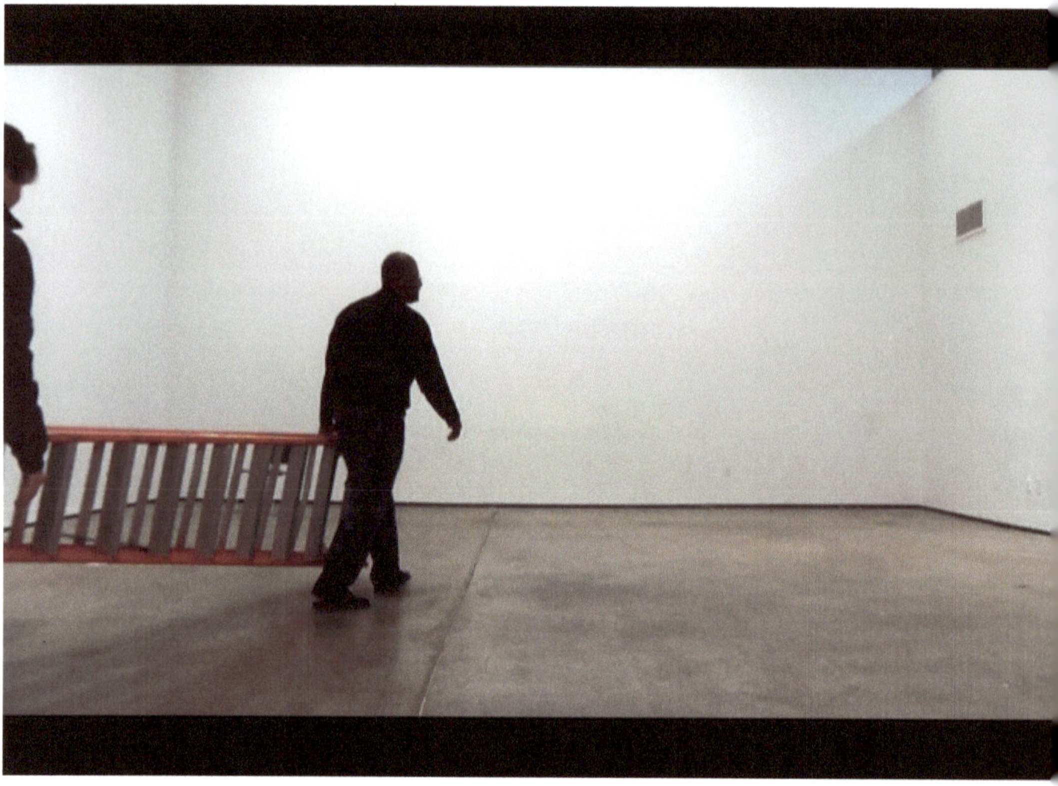

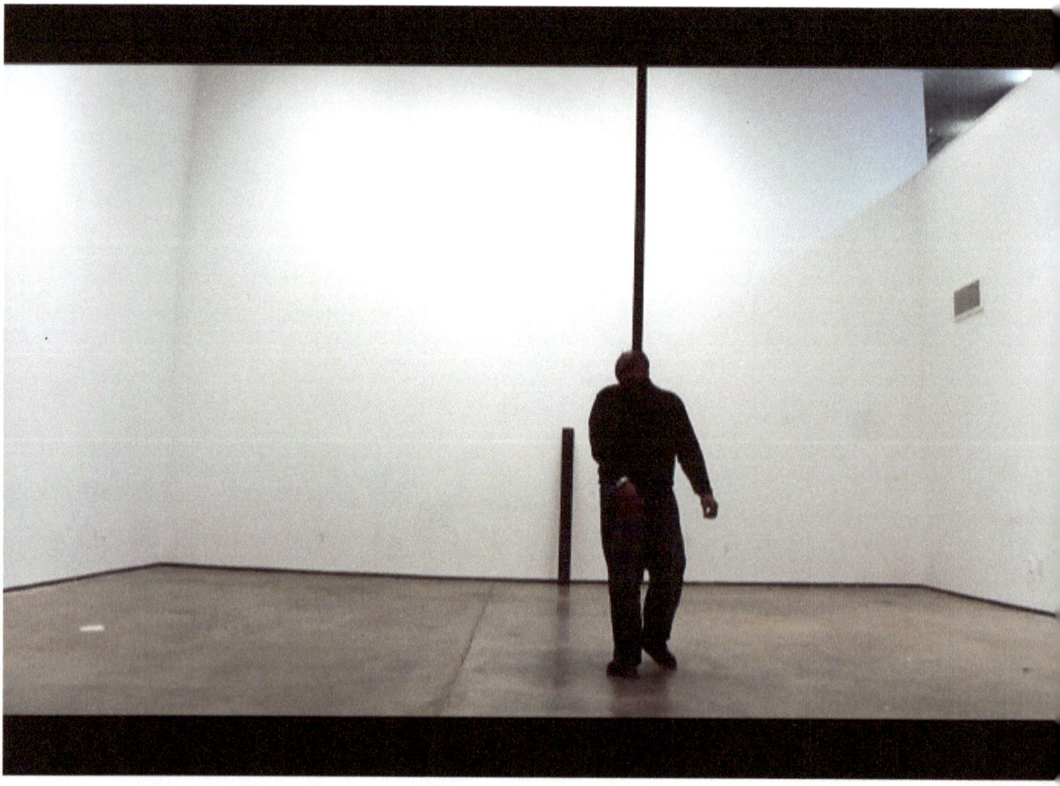

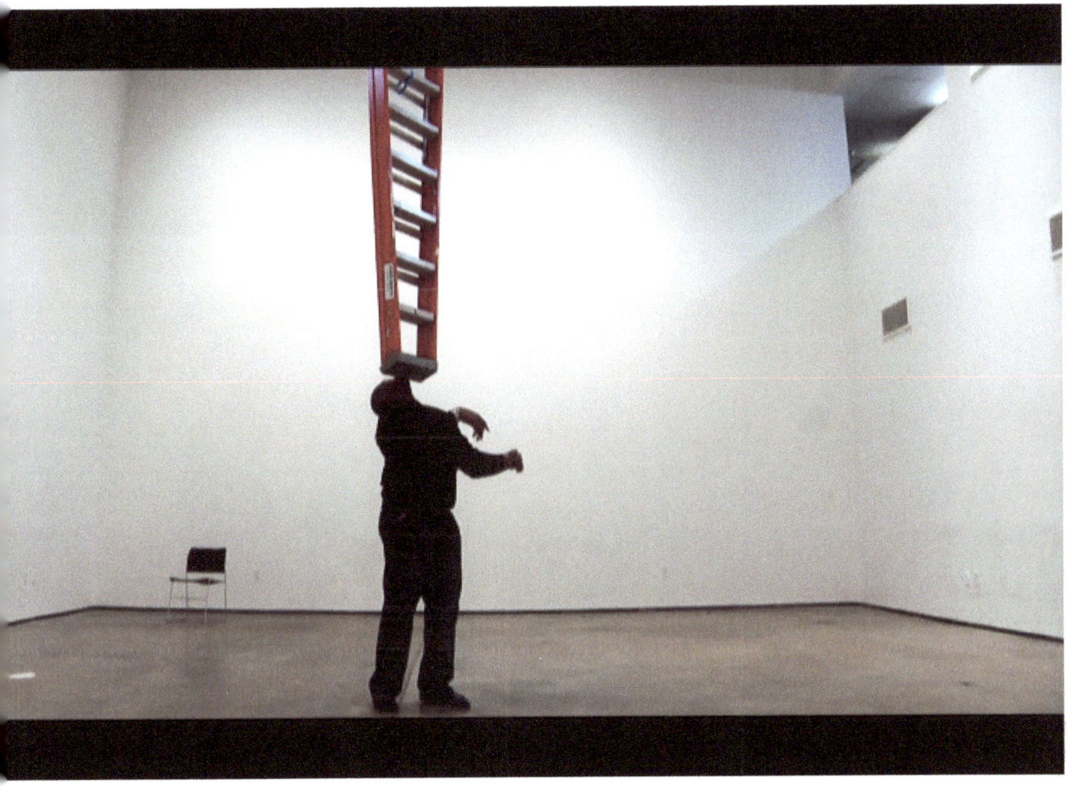

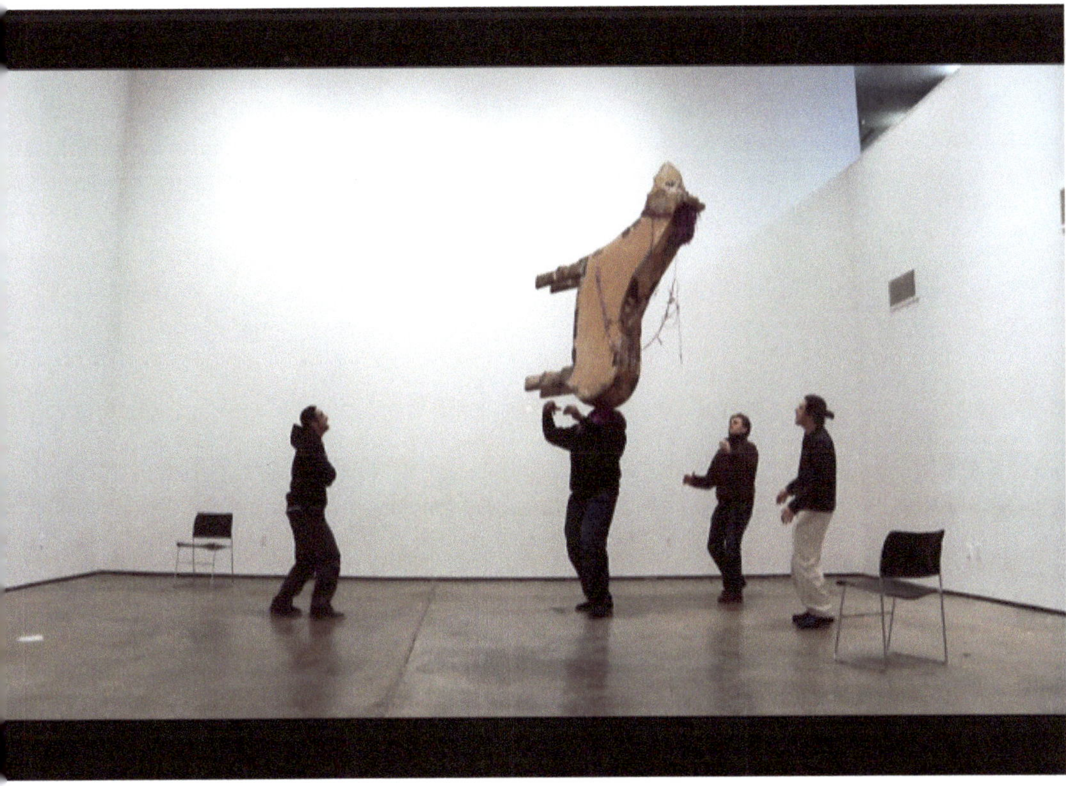

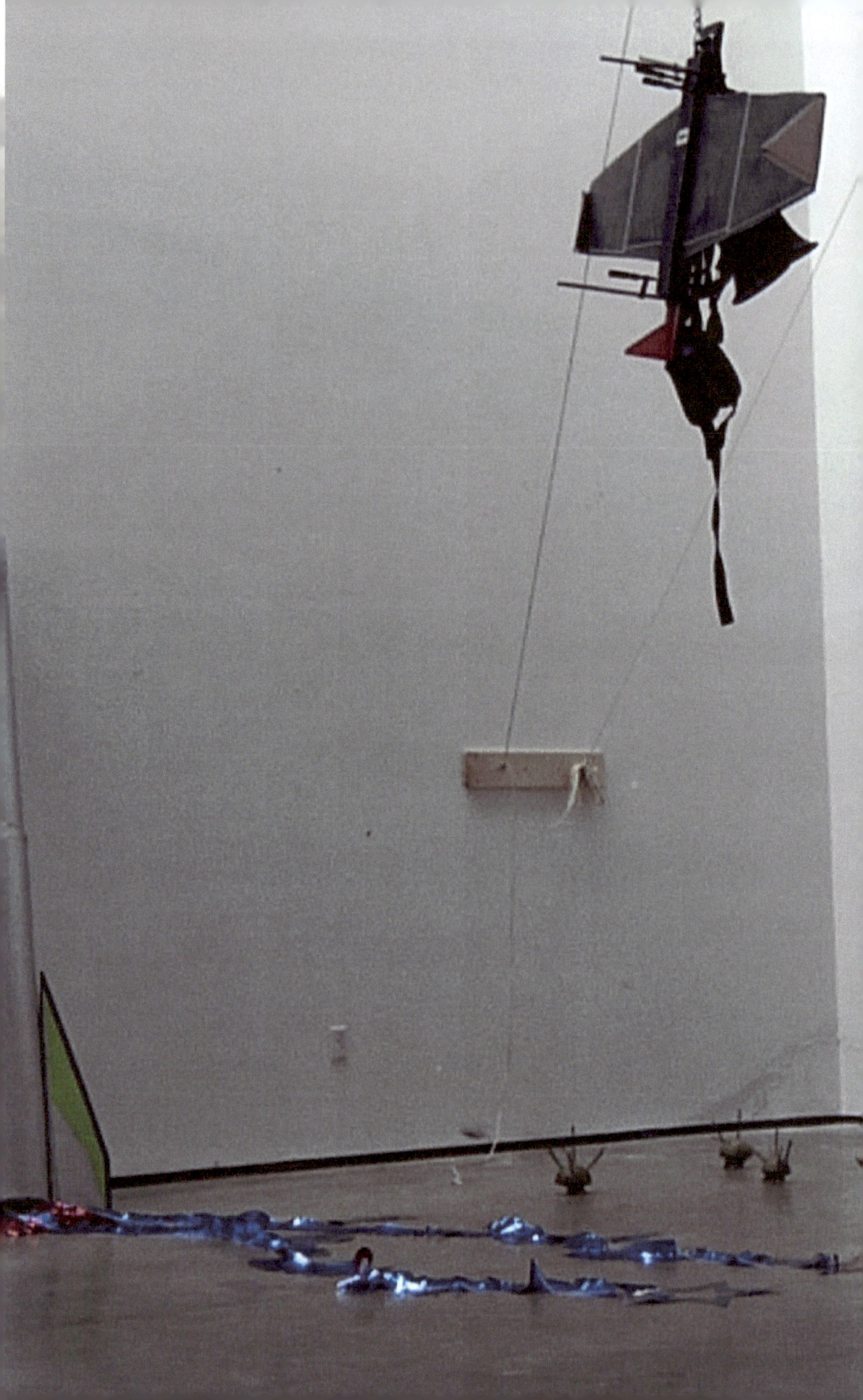

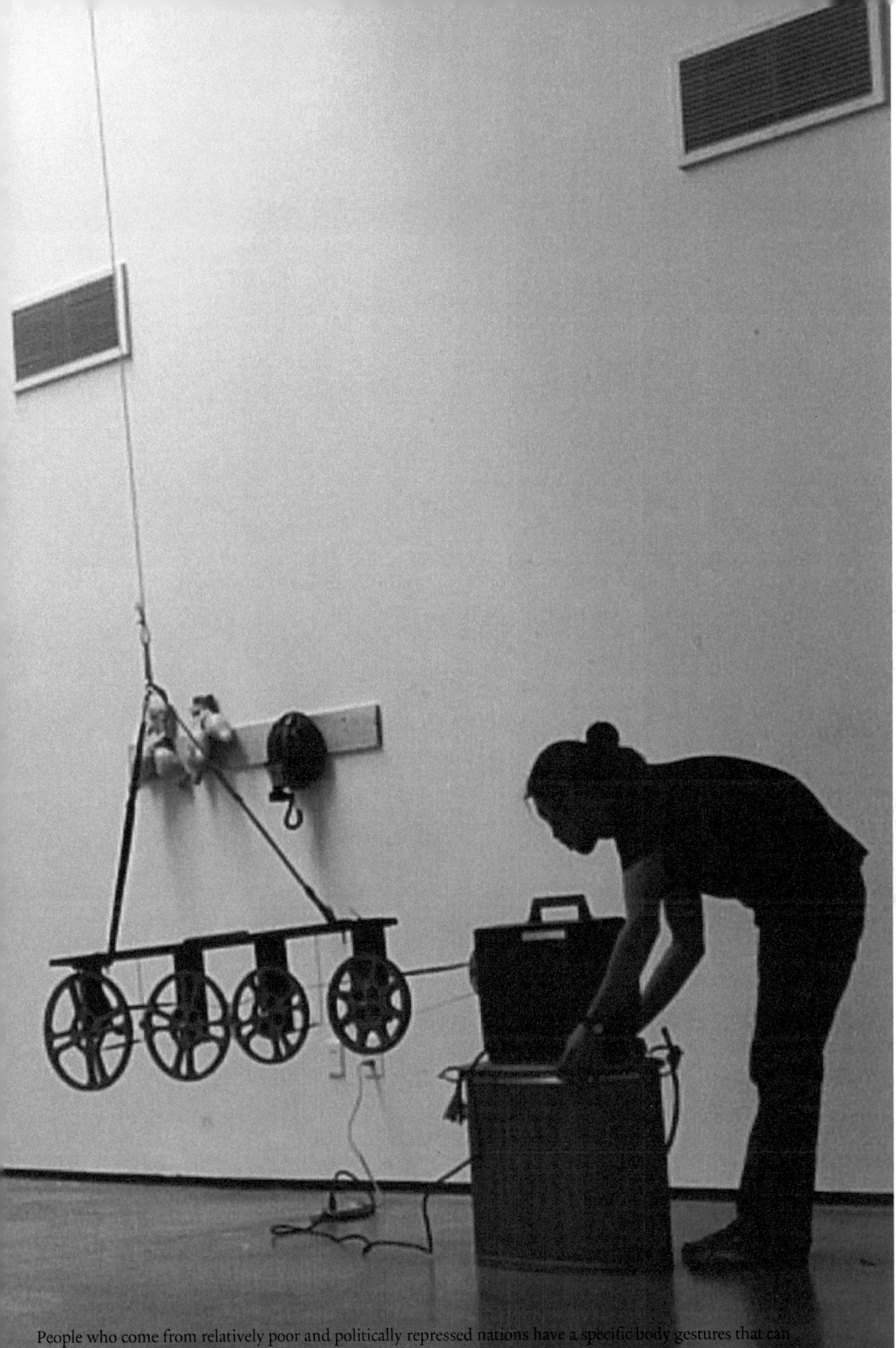

People who come from relatively poor and politically repressed nations have a specific body gestures that can only be understood as a pressure of inferiority.

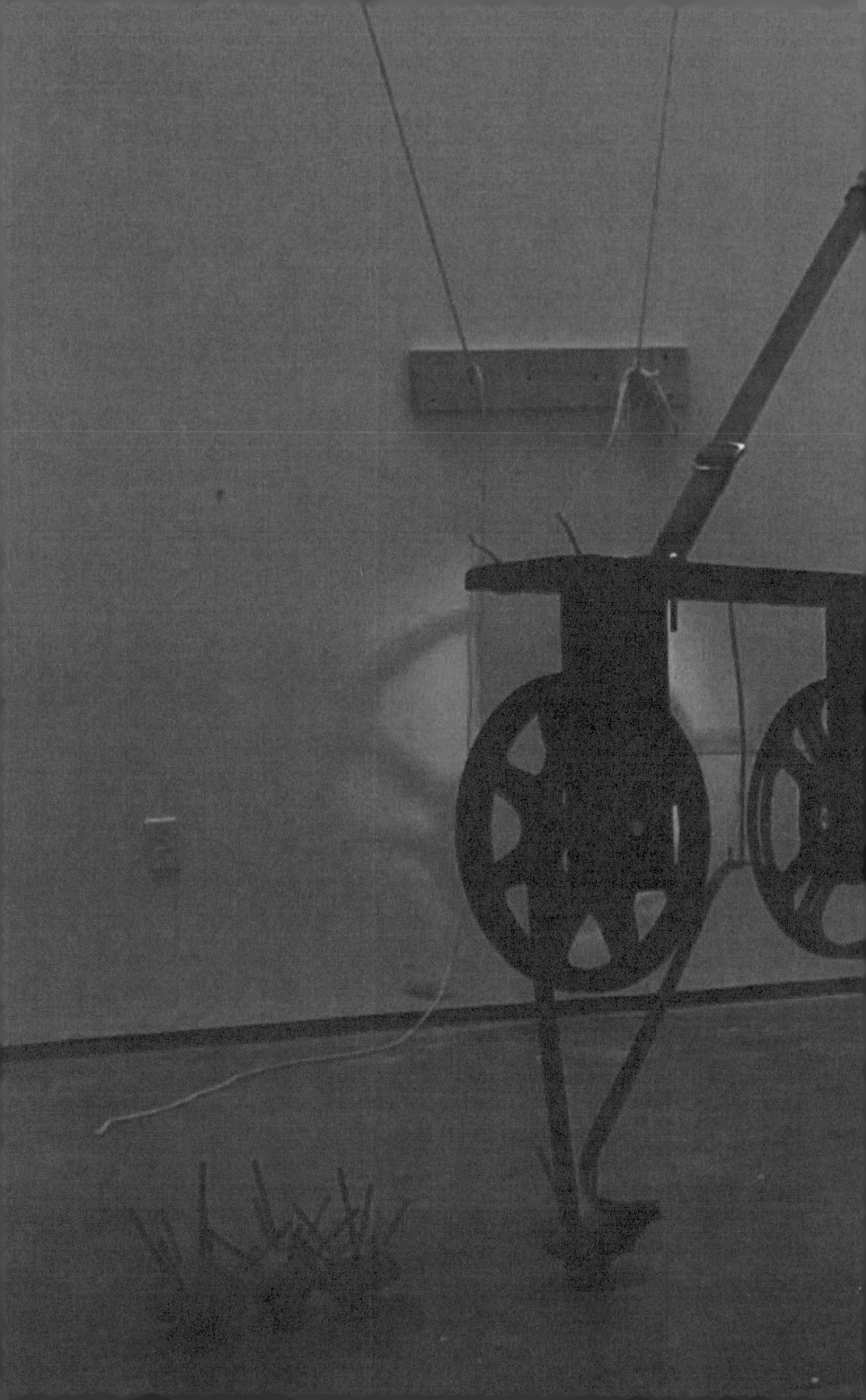

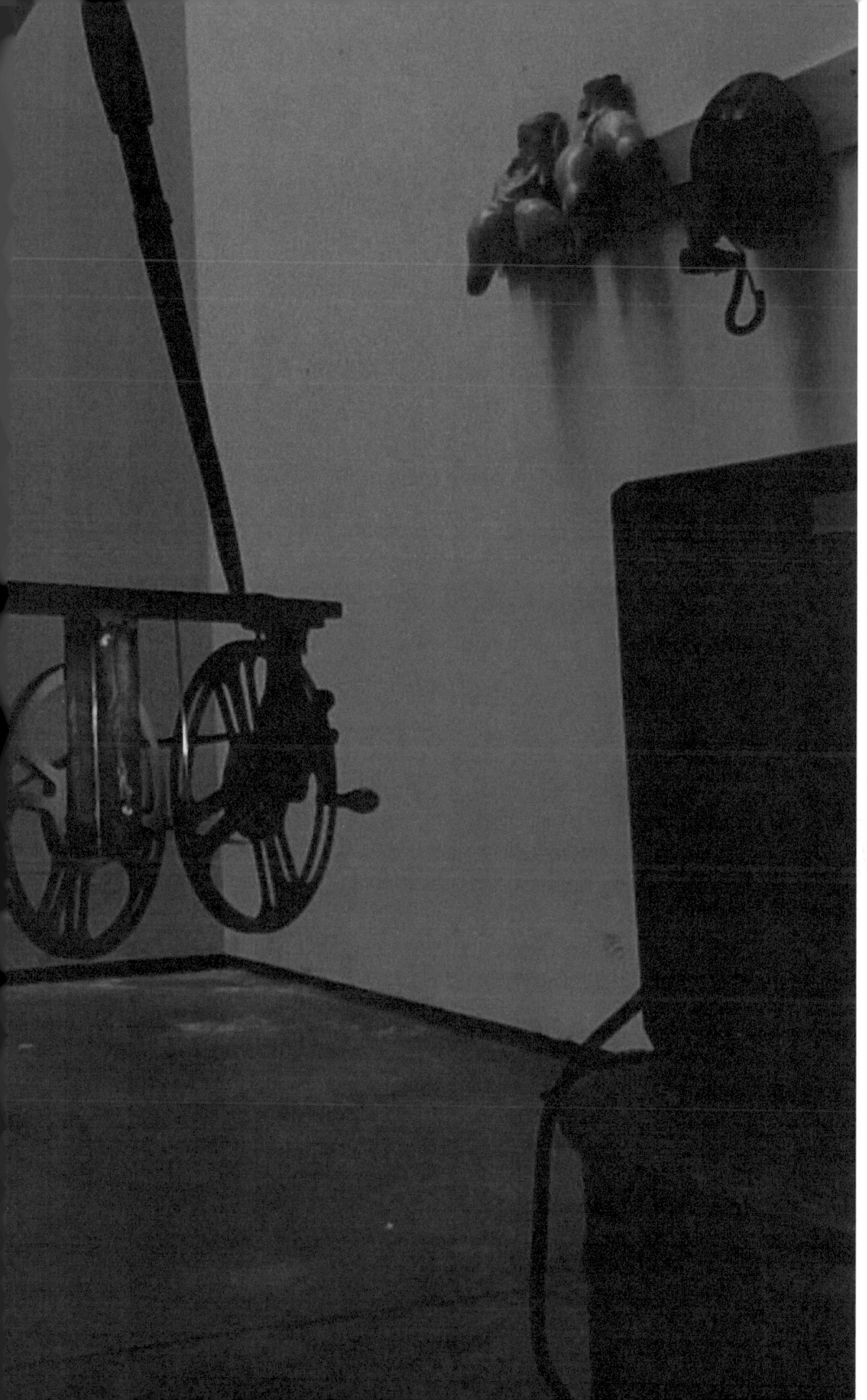

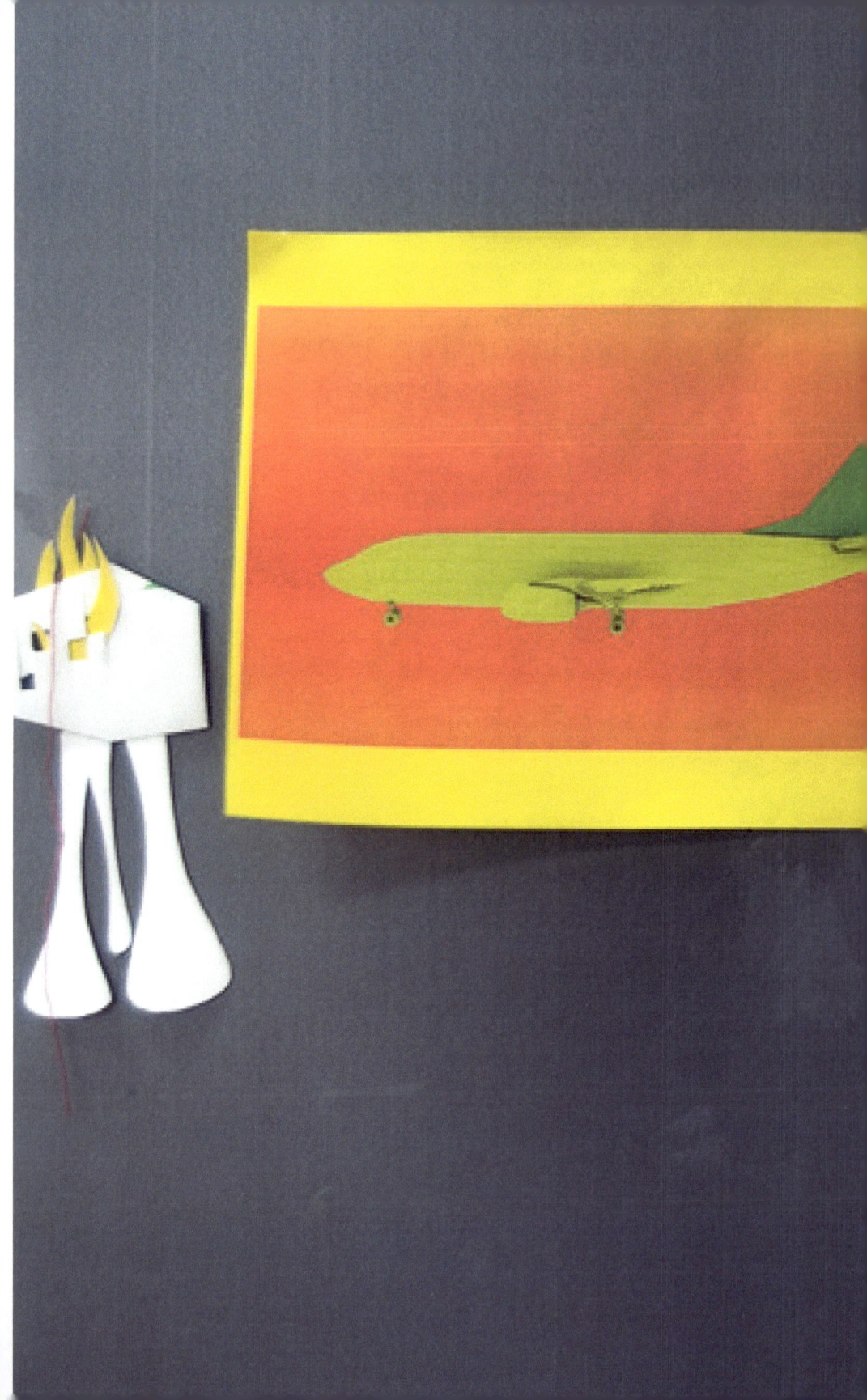

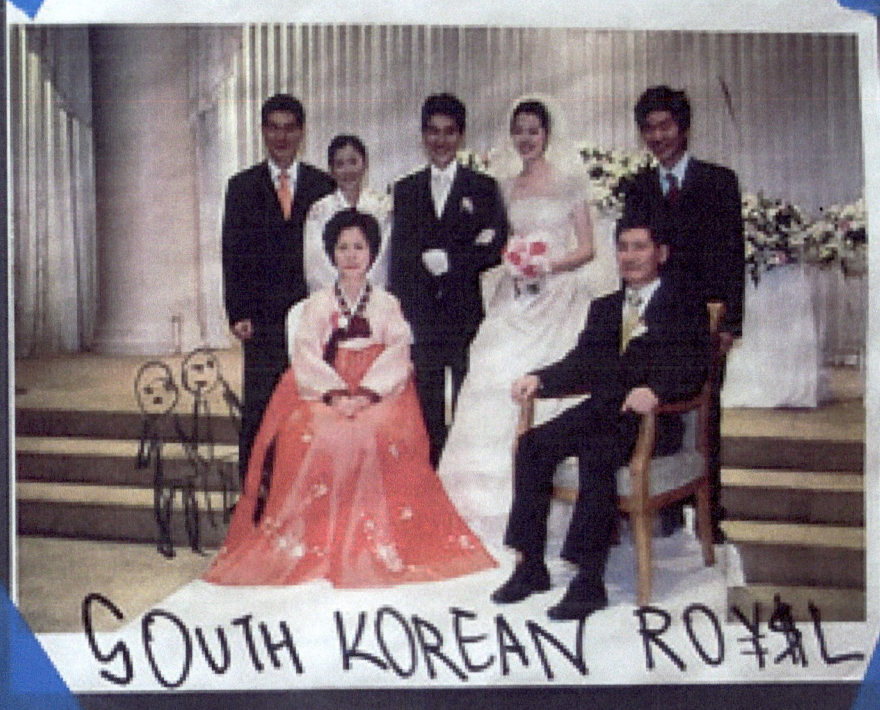

SOUTH KOREAN ROYAL

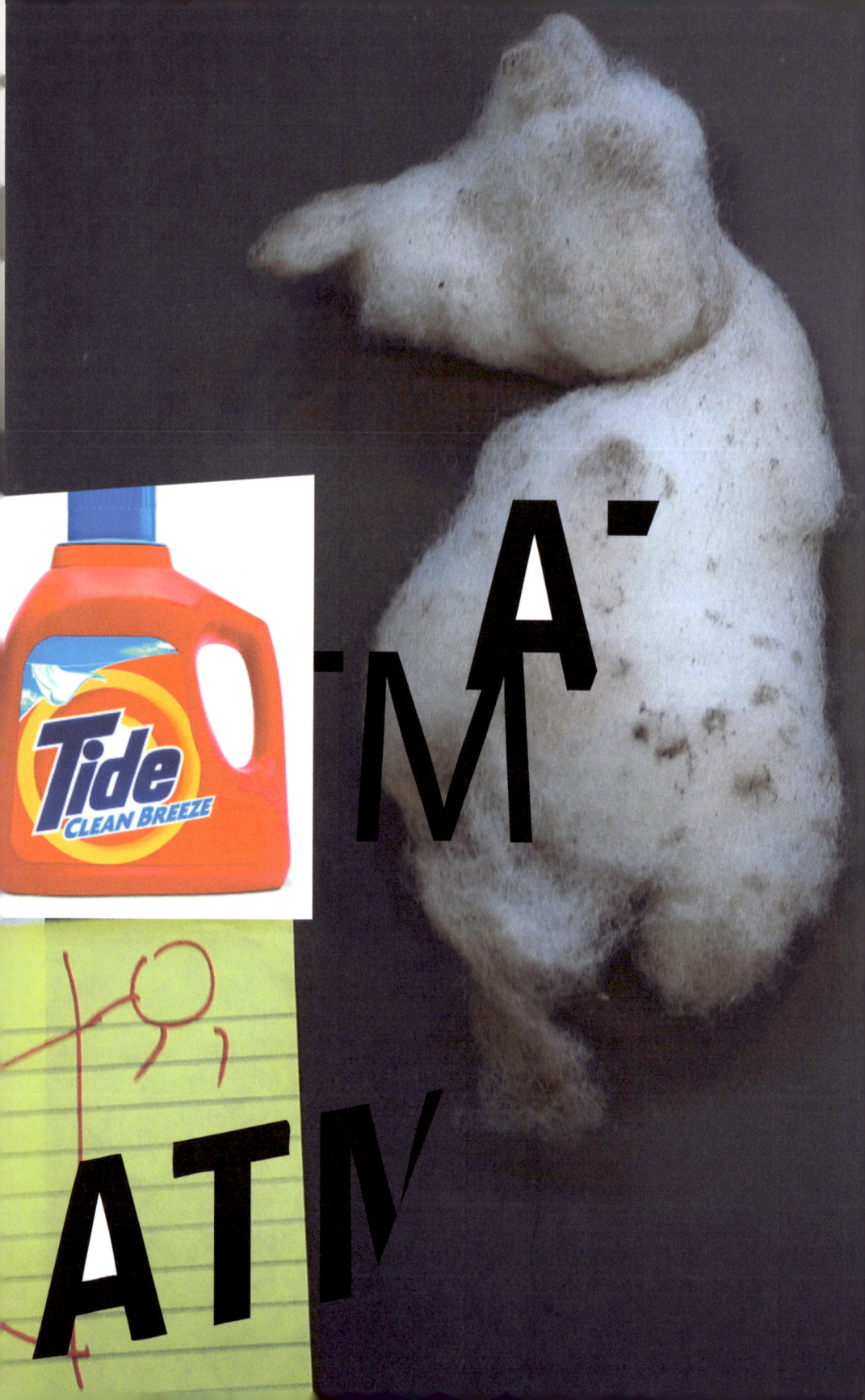

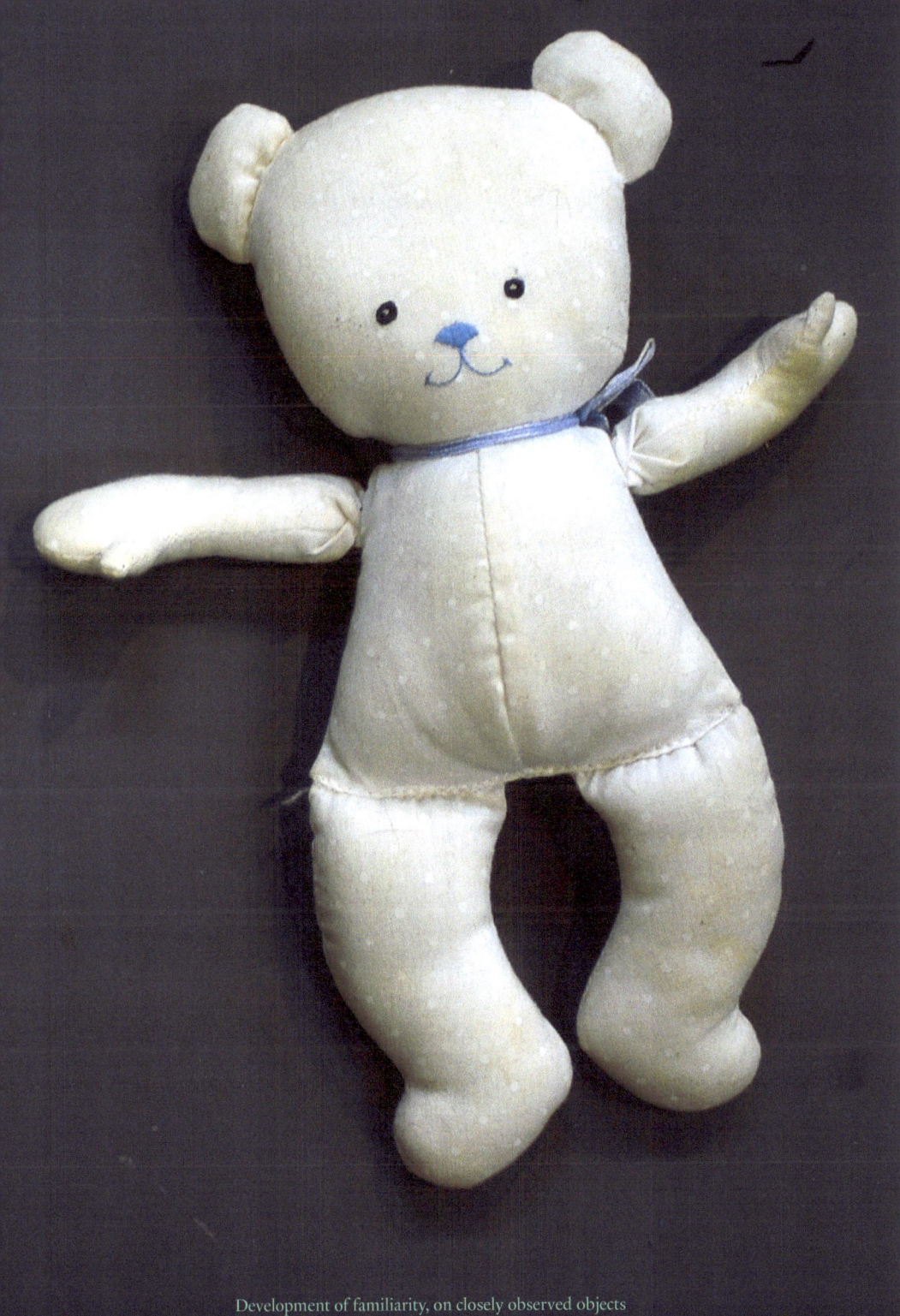

Development of familiarity, on closely observed objects

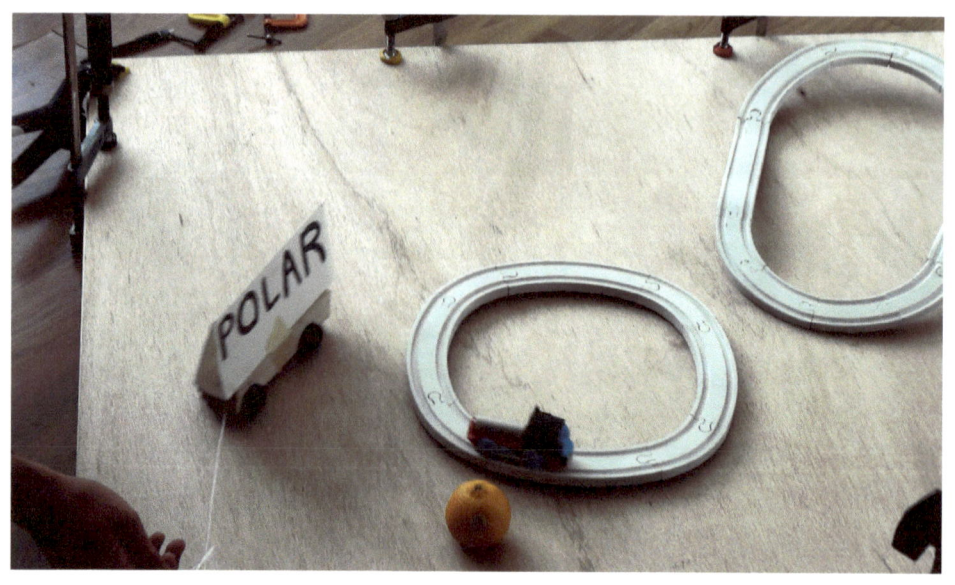

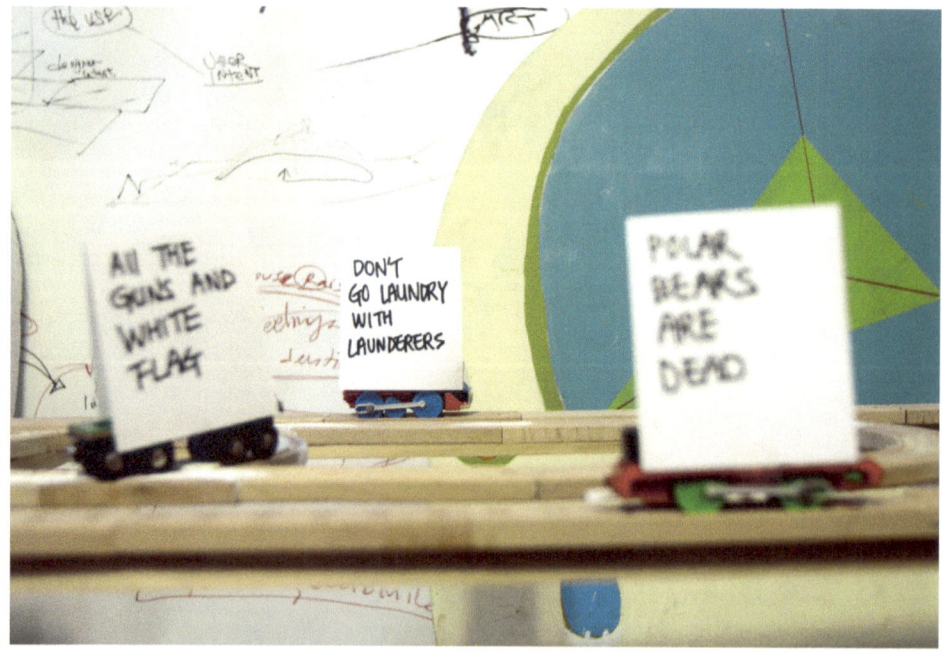

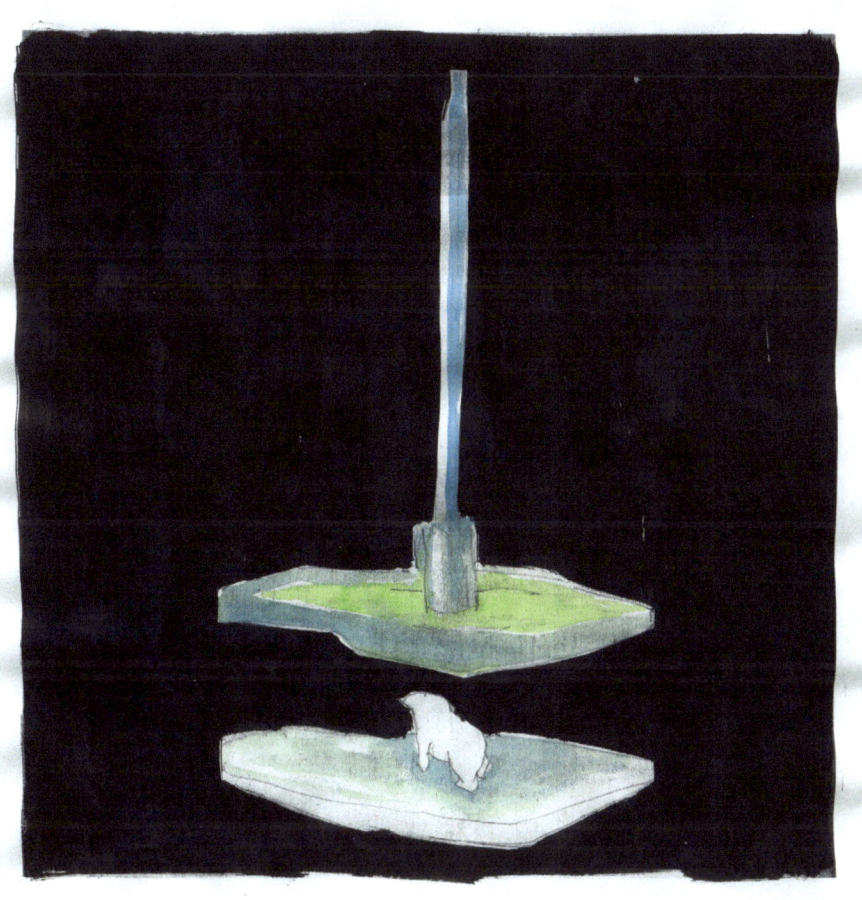

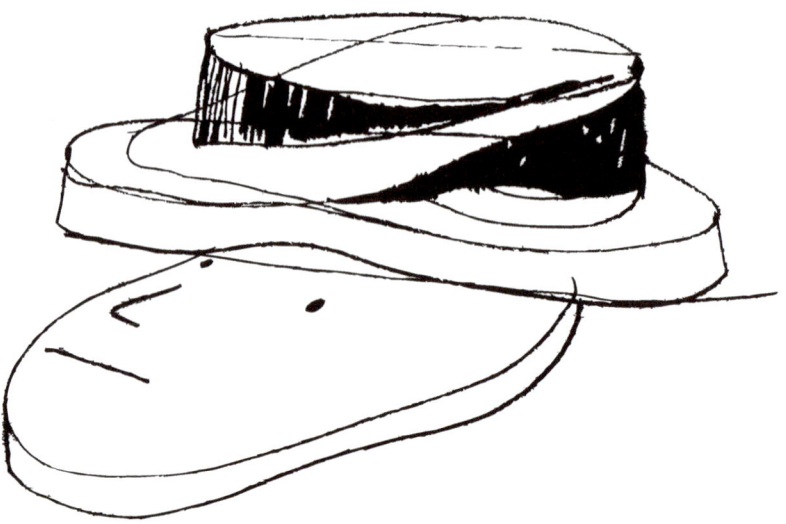

In the mind map of 'Boredom requires charisma'
arrows are pointing to wrong places, time line is
messed up and the links are broken.

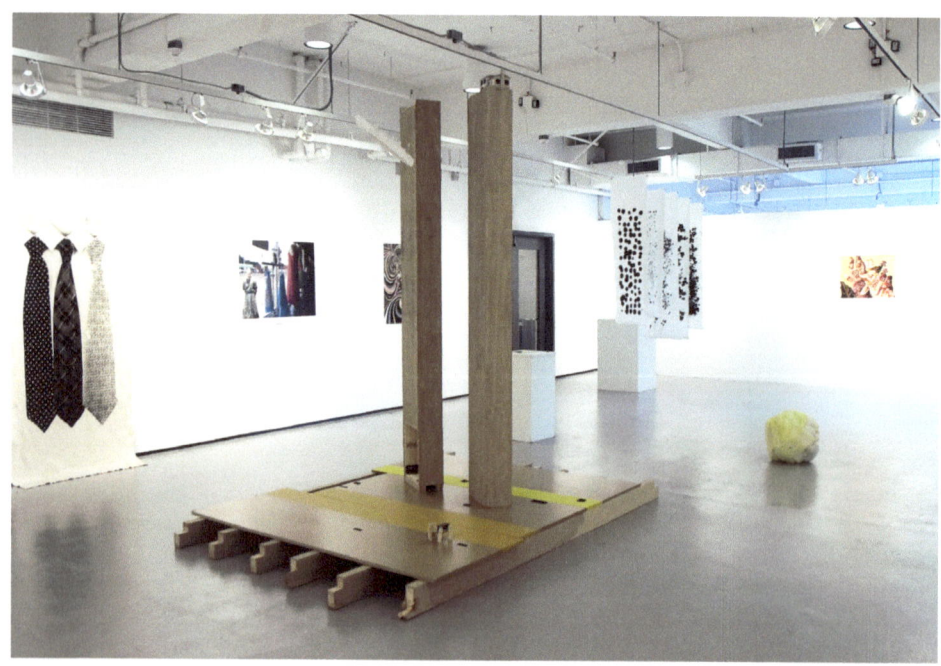

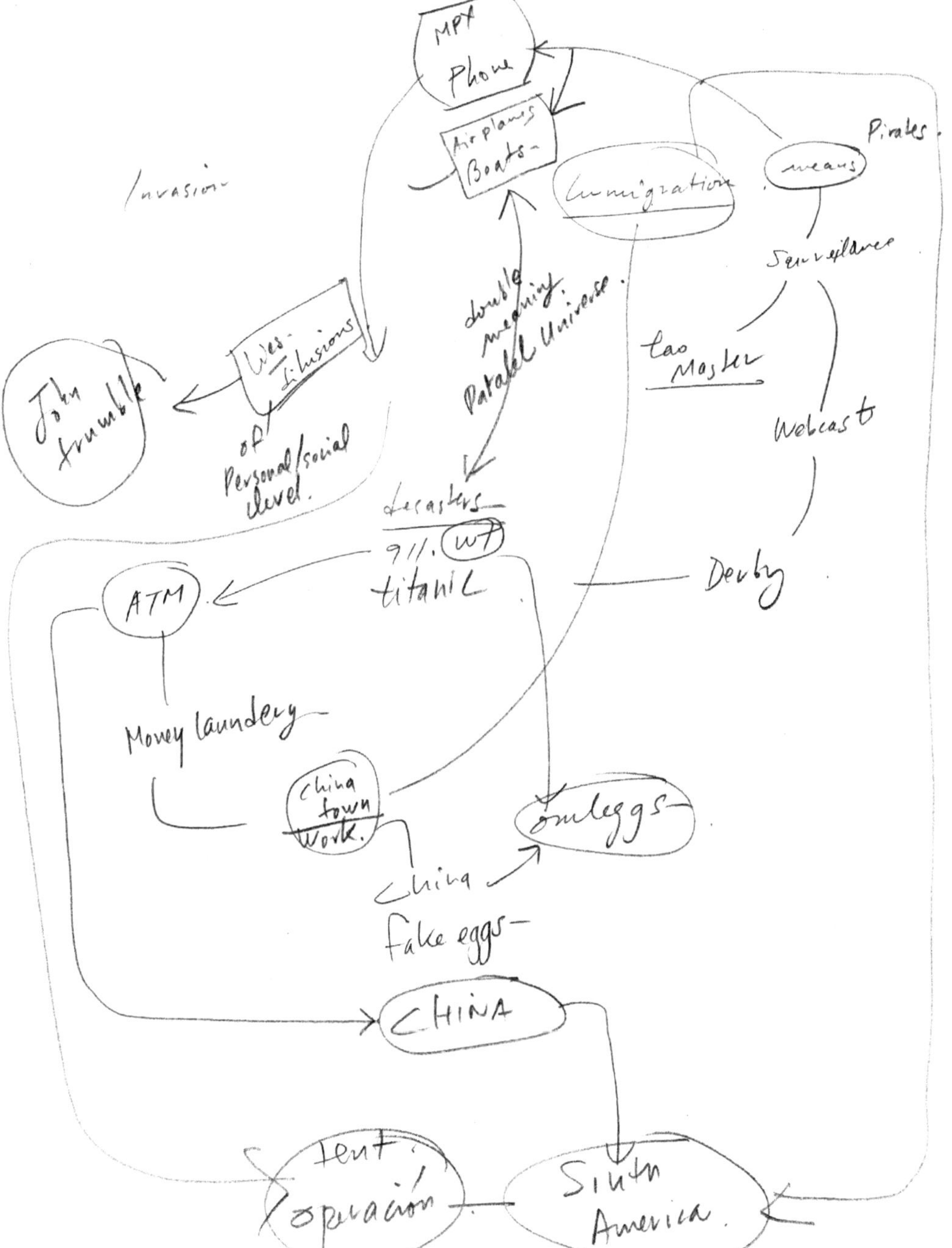

Invasion

MPX
Phone

Airplanes
Boats~

Immigration

means

Pirates.

Surveillance

Uses
Illusions

John
trumble

double
meaning:
Parallel Universe.

of
Personal/social
level.

Tao
Master

Webcast

disasters
9/1. WTC
titanic

Derby

ATM

Money laundery

china
town
Work.

Tom leggs

china

fake eggs~

CHINA

tent.
opiración

South
America.

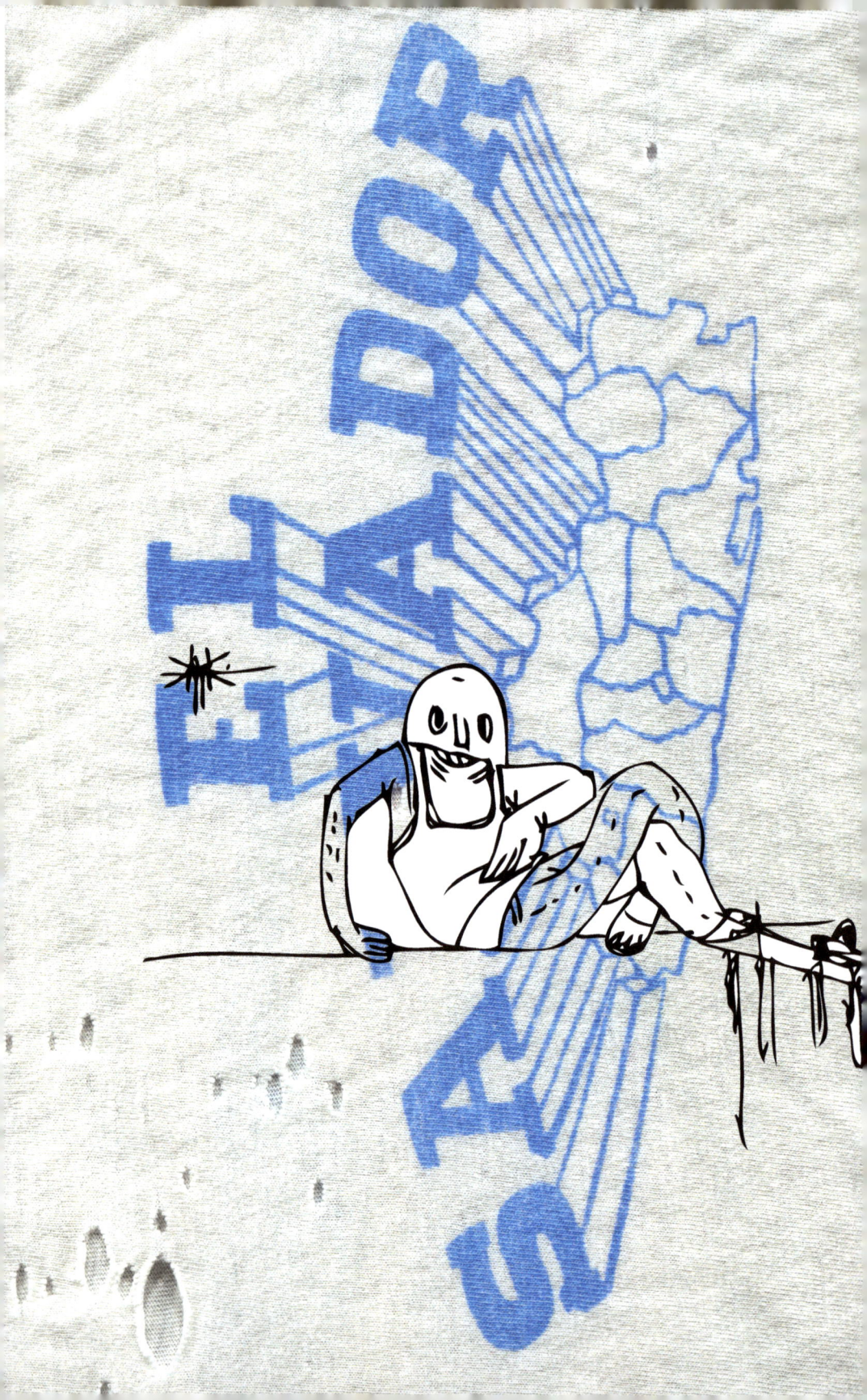

Six Dimensional Artist Profile
Artist: Cheon Pyo Lee

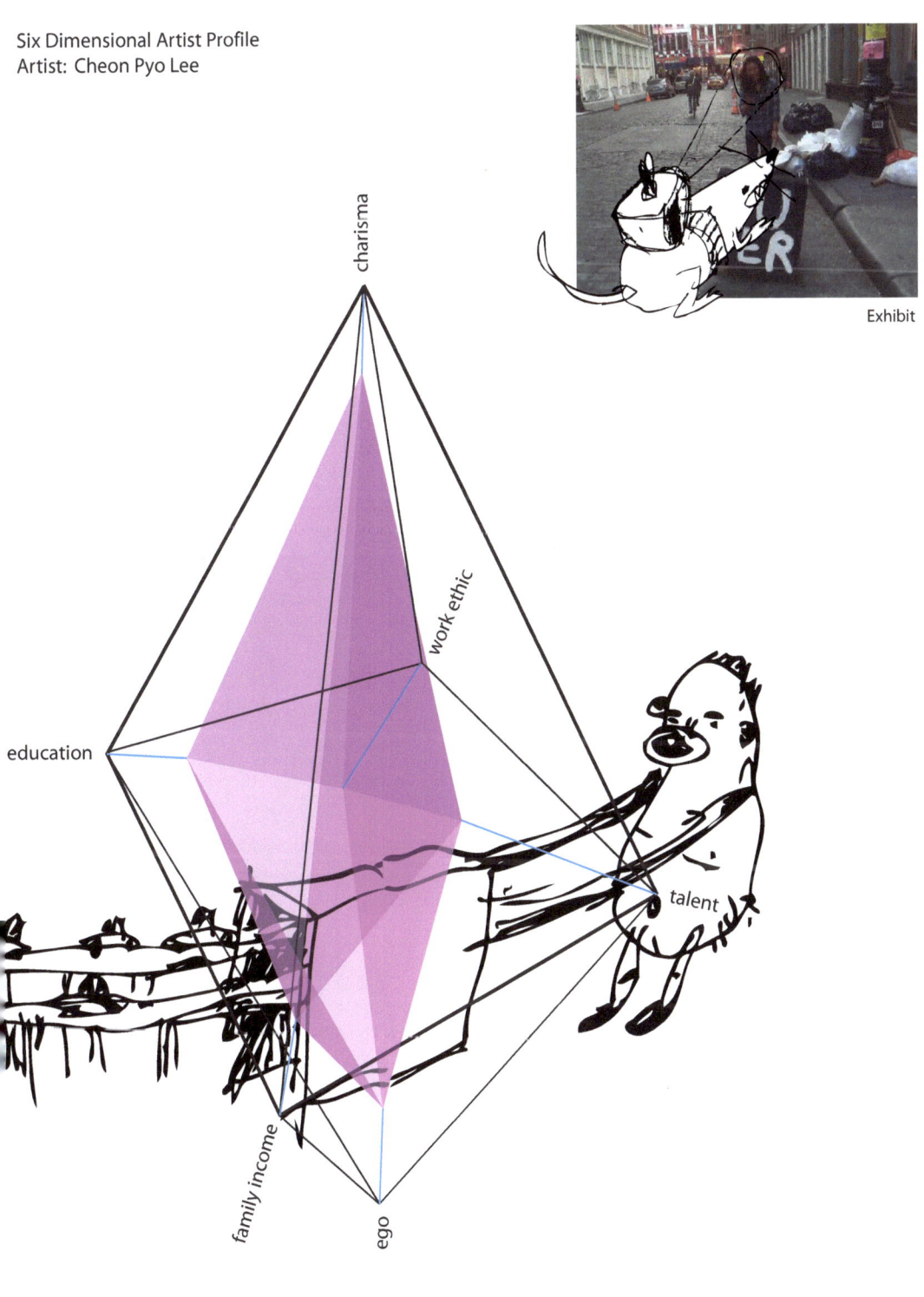

Exhibit

charisma

work ethic

education

talent

family income

ego

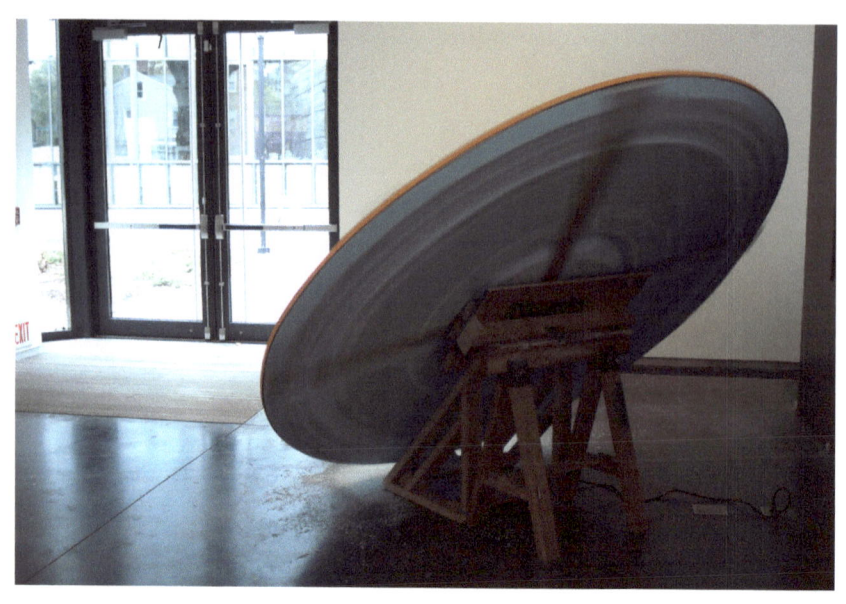

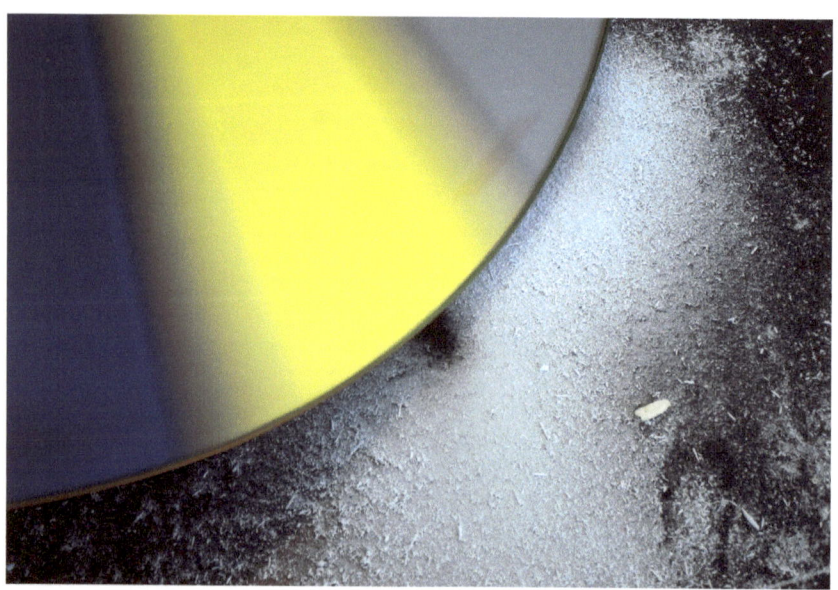

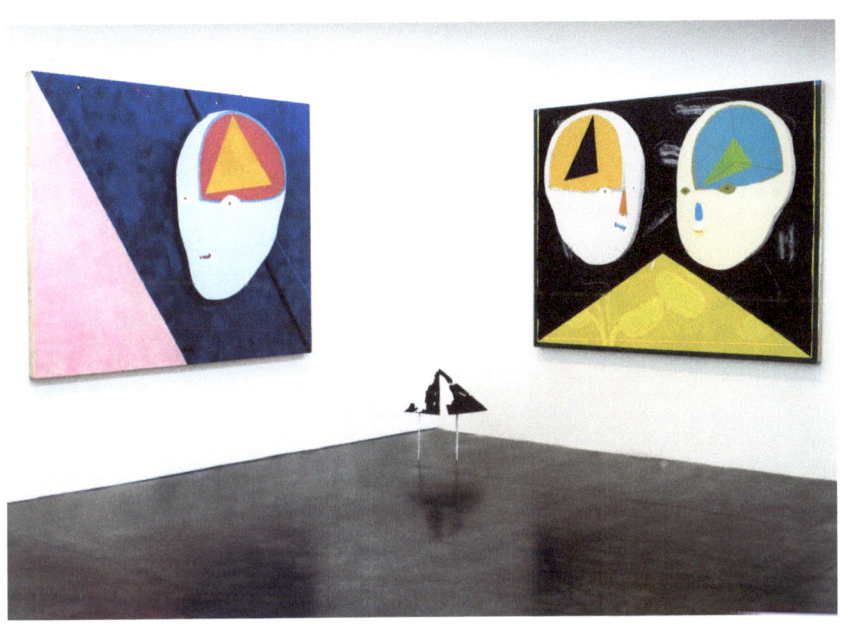

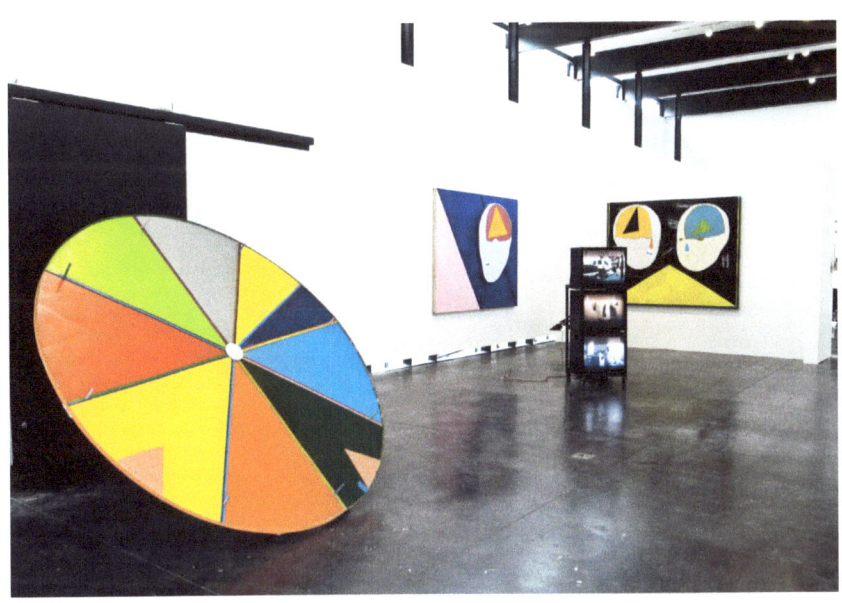

COMU

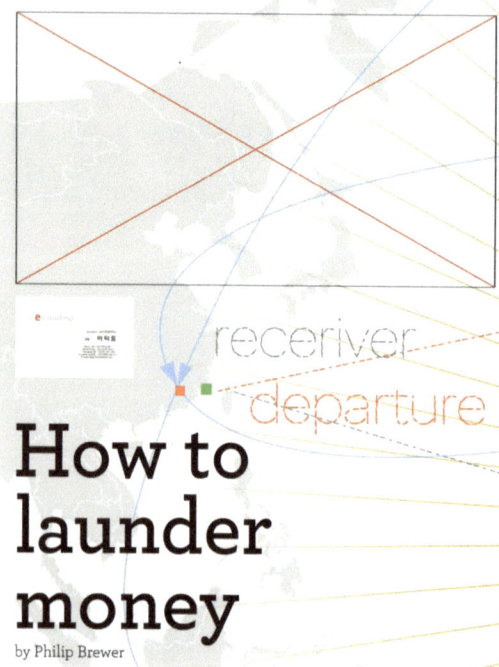

receriver

departure

How to launder money

by Philip Brewer

Modern Money Laundering

The other thing sometimes called money laundering is when you have some big lump of cash that you'd rather not have people find out about. Sometimes it's an effort to keep the money from the tax man (literally the opposite of classic money laundering), other times the goal is to keep it from coming to the attention of someone else who might feel like they have some claim to the money-an ex-spouse, a creditor, the guy who owns the land where you found the bag of gold coins in the culvert.

In this kind of money laundering, the point is to make the money disappear. This is the sort of money laundering where you might make use of foreign banks, shell companies, and so on.

There are two parts to these strategies. First, you need to make the money disappear. Second, you need to make it reappear in some gradual fashion that doesn't bring it to the attention of whoever you're trying to hide it from.

Disappearing the money

The easiest way to disappear the money, especially if it's already cash (as opposed to, let's say, silver bullion or a winning lottery ticket) is to just stash it in a safety deposit box. You miss out on any investment income, but it's safe and you know where to find it.

If you really want to be able to invest the money, get it overseas. If it's an amount that you can just carry with you, buy a vacation package to the Cayman Islands or visit your family roots in Europe and take a little side trip to Switzerland or Austria or Liechtenstein.

There are plenty of fancy, complex ways to get the money overseas, that mostly require an accomplice. The most basic is an invoice scam. Establish a business that

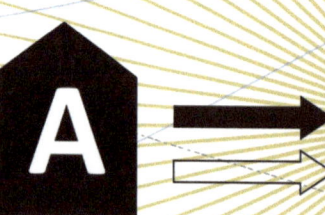

Cheque Fraud.

Cheque (or check) fraud refers to a category of criminal that involve making the unlawful use of cheques in orc illegally acquire or borrow funds that do not exist withi account balance or account-holder's legal ownership. methods involve taking advantage of the float (the between the negotiation of the cheque and its clearan the cheque-writer's bank) to draw out these funds. Spe kinds of cheque fraud include cheque kiting, where f are deposited before the end of the float period to the fraud, and paper hanging, where the float offers opportunity to write fraudulent checks but the accou

ICADO

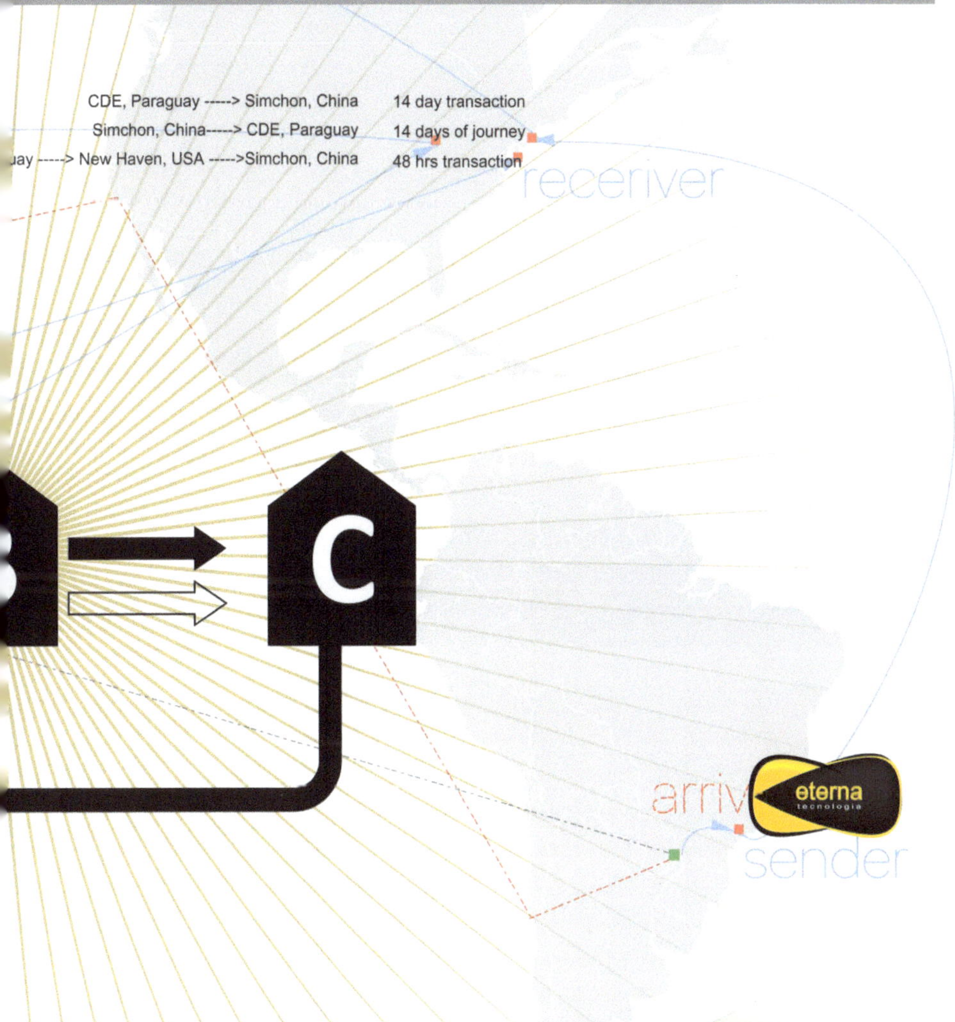

CDE, Paraguay -----> Simchon, China   14 day transaction

Simchon, China-----> CDE, Paraguay   14 days of journey

uay -----> New Haven, USA ----->Simchon, China   48 hrs transaction

receriver

C

arriv **eterna** tecnologia

sender

outh America's
ri-border'
ack on

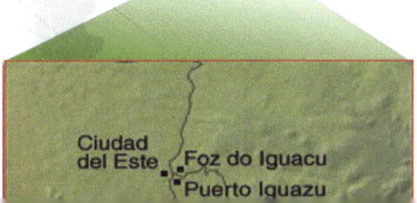

Ciudad
del Este   Foz do Iguacu
            Puerto Iguazu

The other thing sometimes called money laundering is when you have some big lump of cash that you'd rather not have people find out about. Sometimes it's an effort to keep the money from the tax man (literally the opposite of classic money laundering), other times the goal is to keep it from coming to the attention of someone else who might feel like they have some claim to the money–an ex-spouse, a creditor, the guy who owns the land where you found the bag of gold coins in the culvert.

In this kind of money laundering, the point is to make the money disappear. This is the sort of money laundering where you might make use of foreign banks, shell companies, and so on.

There are two parts to these strategies. First, you need to make the money disappear. Second, you need to make it reappear in some gradual fashion that doesn't bring it to the attention of whoever you're trying to hide it from.

Disappearing the money

The easiest way to disappear the money, especially if it's already cash (as opposed to, let's say, silver bullion or a winning lottery ticket) is to just stash it in a safety deposit box. You miss out on any investment income, but it's safe and you know where to find it.

If you really want to be able to invest the money, get it overseas. If it's an amount that you can just carry with you, buy a vacation package to the Cayman Islands or visit your family roots in Europe and take a little side trip to Switzerland or Austria or Liechtenstein.

There are plenty of fancy, complex ways to get the money overseas, that mostly require an accomplice. The most basic is an invoice scam. Establish a business that imports or exports something. Meet with your customer or supplier and arrange with him to either over-pay or under-bill, and then to have your counterpart deposit (most of) the excess into your foreign bank account. An ongoing scheme is good, because the guy knows that the lucrative cash flow will stop if you find out the money isn't getting deposited as it should, but you can also work this as a one-shot deal if your counterpart can be trusted.

Banks used to help their good customers get money discretely overseas, but nowadays there are a bunch of laws against such things, and bankers are particularly averse to going to jail for their customers. Expect them to refused to get involved and to rat you out.

Reappearing the money

If you've got the money overseas somewhere, bring it back in some way that makes it legit. The easiest would be to create an overseas company that then hires you to do something. You do whatever it is and send an invoice whenever you want some cash. You can also reverse the invoice scam that let you get the money overseas in the first place--now you under-pay (or over-bill), while making up the difference out of your foreign bank account. A third option is a fake loan where you 'borrow' the money and then simply fail to pay the money back.

Instant disappear-reappear cycles

All these money laundering crimes have large fines and long prison sentences. I recommend against them. I also recommend against expecting anyone else to be willing to commit these crimes for you--expect that any accomplices are really either Federal agents, or else will call Federal agents at the first opportunity.

Cheque Fraud.

Cheque (or check) fraud refers to a category of crimin... that involve making the unlawful use of cheques in o... illegally acquire or borrow funds that do not exist with... account balance or account-holder's legal ownership... methods involve taking advantage of the float (the... between the negotiation of the cheque and its clear... the cheque-writer's bank) to draw out these funds. S... kinds of cheque fraud include cheque kiting, where... are deposited before the end of the float period to... the fraud, and paper hanging, where the float offe... opportunity to write fraudulent checks but the acco... never replenished.

The most notorious 'bad cheque artist' of the 20th ce... Frank Abagnale, devised a scheme to put incorrect... numbers at the bottom of the cheque he wrote, so tha... would be routed to the incorrect Federal Reserve Ba... clearing. This allowed him to work longer in one area... his criminal activity was detected.

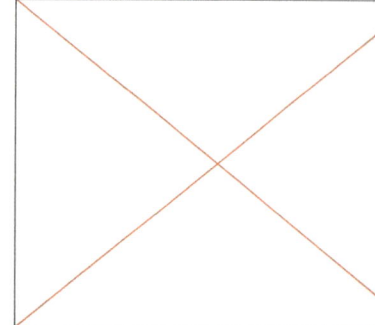

The Black Capital To Be Laundered
True Beneficial Owner accumulates $27 Million in undeclared revenue (i.e. black capital) in the U.S.

Laundering Link #1: The Liberian Corp.
True Beneficial Owner secretly forms
a Liberian shell corporation.

Laundering Link #2: The Curacao Bank
True Beneficial Owner deposits the $27 million into the Liberian corporation's bank account in Curacao.

Laundering Link #3: Final Washing In Amsterdam
An Amsterdam bank loans True Beneficial Owner $26 million. The loan however, is fully collateralized by True Beneficial Owner's earlier $27 million Curacao deposit and is "back-to-back".

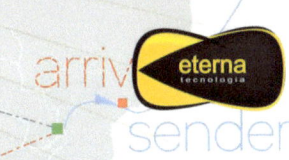

outh America's ri-border' ack on rrorism radar

ke Boettcher CNN

ovember 8, 2002 Posted: 7:20 PM EST (0020 GMT)

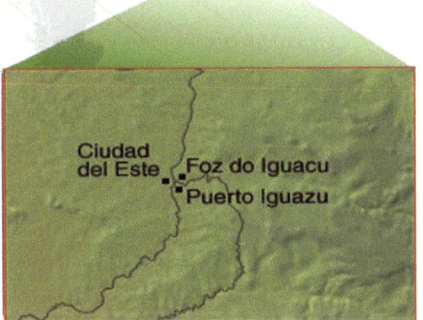

has learned from coalition intelligence sources that several top terrorist
ves met recently in the area -- where the borders of Argentina, Brazil
raguay intersect -- to plan attacks against U.S. and Israeli targets in the
n hemisphere. (Map of the tri-border region)

s said the meetings, which took place in and around Ciudad del Este,
ttended by representatives of Hezbollah and other groups sympathetic to
bin Laden's al Qaeda terrorist network.

eeks ago, Argentina's security agencies issued a strong terrorist warning.
indications of the threat came from intelligence sources in the Middle
ho told CNN of a new terrorist effort aimed at U.S. and Israeli interests
ordinated by a man named Imad Mugniyeh.

ina's Toma met recently with intelligence officials in Washington
uss the possibility of a new terrorist offensive launched from South
ca.

vas a central theme discussed in recent trips to Washington," Toma said.
is a direct correlation between terrorism here and the U.S."

tine intelligence documents obtained by CNN last year spell out links
en those groups and mosques and businesses in the area. Hezbollah
lamic Jihad are Arab-based groups which have directed the bulk of their
es against Israel. Gamaa al Islamiya, an Egyptian group, has publicly
tself with al Qaeda.

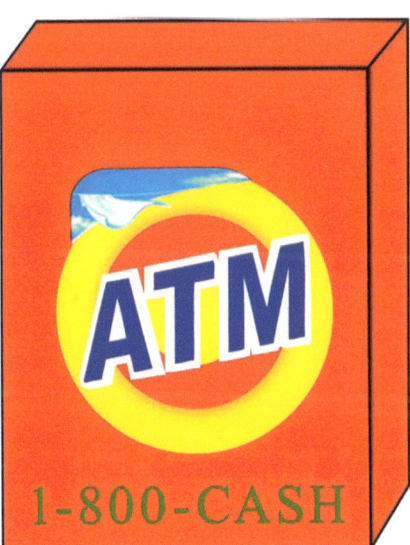

ngs about terrorist activity in the tri-border region are not new. The lush
region is known for its porous borders and thriving black markets.
gion quickly fell under the anti-terrorism dragnet cast after September
days after the attacks, police in Paraguay raided several businesses and
ed up 20 suspects, 14 of whom were later released.

tine officials point to more evidence they say indicates terrorist activity
tri-border area -- thousands of U.S. dollars bearing stamps from Lebanese
cy exchange banks, tens of thousands of dollars in phony bills, and receipts
vire transfers made between the tri-border area and the Middle East.

raeli Embassy in Buenos Aires, Argentina, was bombed in 1992.

international intelligence agencies have focused on the tri-border region
the war on terror began, many of the people they were looking for may
noved on.

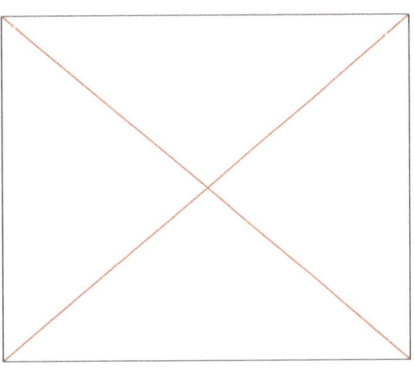

tina's counter-terrorism police assert that terrorist operatives have
sed east, to the remote jungles of Brazil and to Brazil's financial capital, Sao
and west, to the free trade zone of Iquique in Chile's northern desert.
ear, U.S. officials requested that Chile investigate terrorist activity in
e. Police there recently seized 48 fake Pakistani passports, which they
e were destined for use by terrorists.

s Ingrid Arnesen contributed to this report.

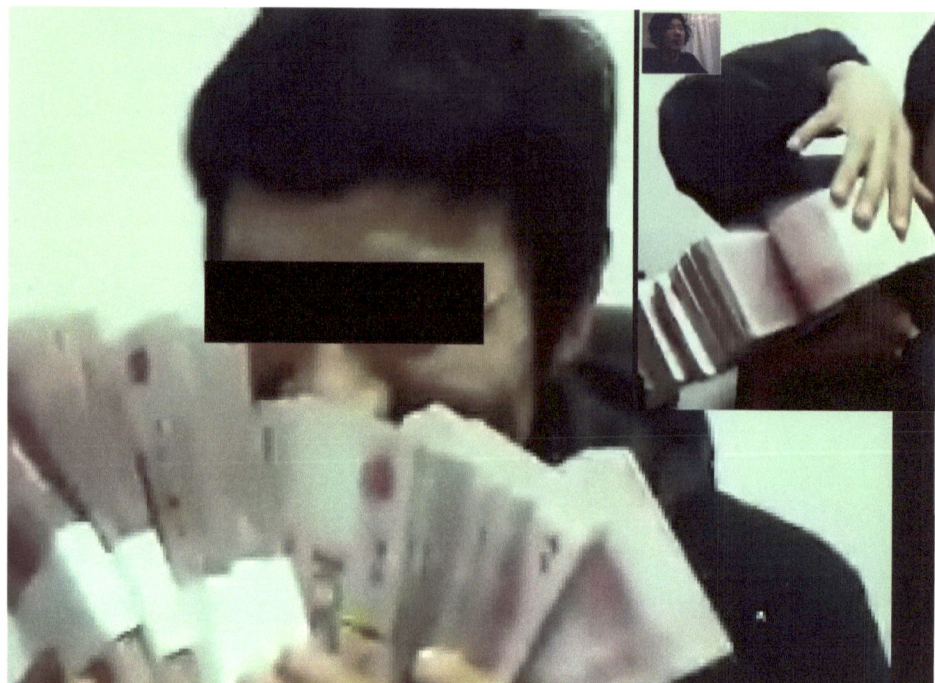

By counting money, it becomes more money.

The only weakness of money was its physicality. Paper money are heavy and bulky. In an advanced capitalist society the currency is digitized. Money becomes transcendental. It is the closest thing to the God.

Y te vas o te quedas? Are you going or staying?
Y te vas o te quedas? Are you going or staying?

Cajero: dos pesos cincuenta.
Yo: Manolo, te vas o te quedas?
Manolo, te vas o te quedas?

Manolo es mi mejor amigo, mi Kuate.
El tiene dos hermano como yo, y cada uno de ellos estan con mis hermanos. Los tres hermanos fueron bautizados cuando eramos pequeños.

Cuando cada uno de nostros cumplimos quince los viejos nos dieron dos legalos. MaMa nos dio una cadena de oro con la Santissima, diciendo que, por si acaso hubieramos perdido como volver a casa, que la santa nos iva guiar. La cadena pesaba casi 100 gramos, valiendo un pasage a casa desde cualquier lugar del mundo.

Y te vas o te quedas? Are you going or staying?
Y te vas o te quedas? Are you going or staying?

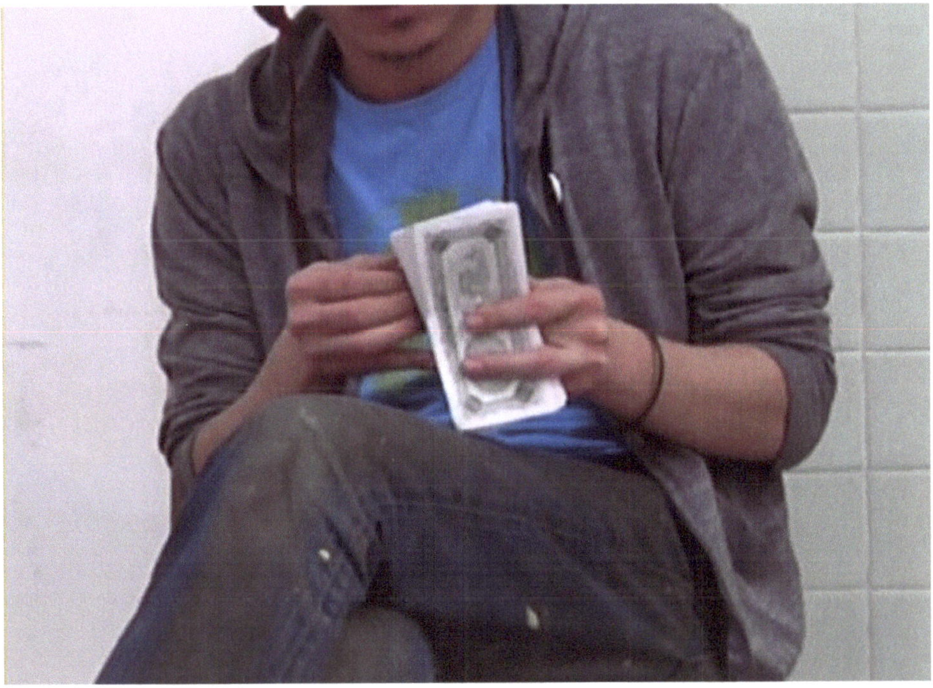

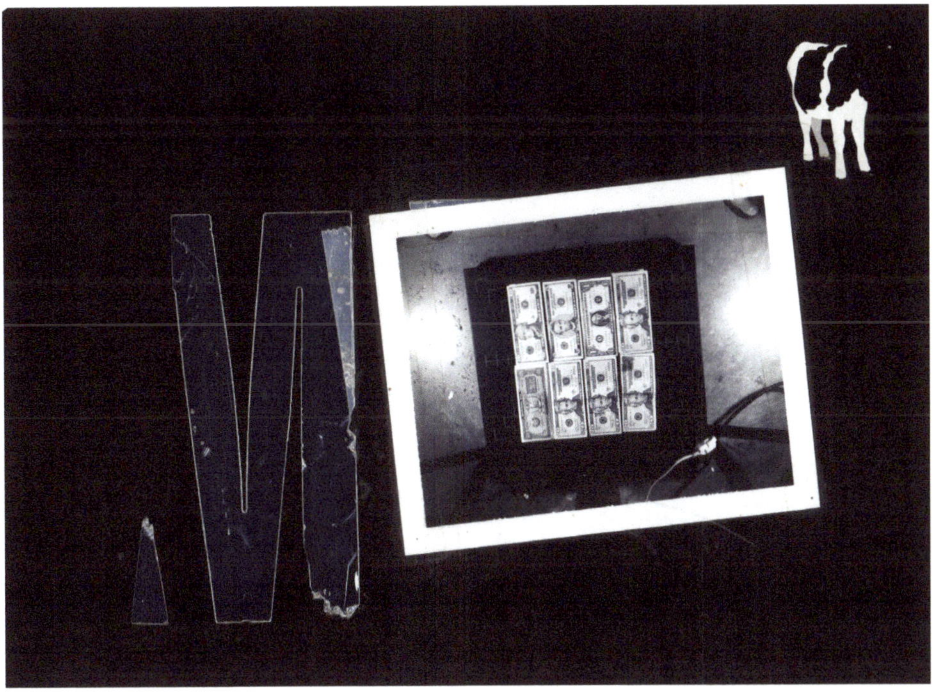

INTERVIEW

S: Mr Lee we are from IRS, Can you confirm your name? we have couple
of questions about your bank activities, are you willing to cooperate?

L: Yes, my name is cheon pyo lee, how can I help you? what is this about?

S: We noticed several activities in your account that we decided it is
suspicious, what do you do mr Lee?

L: I'm an artist I rescently graduated from yale, I've got my MFA from there.

S: Do you have any business with WWW lumber? (This is one of the
companies who deposited the money to my acc) do you recognize it?

L: They are my brothers customer, they wired me the money so I can send
 it to my brother.

S: So You were getting money for your brother?

L: yes, sometimes people pay me here,and I wire the money for him.

S: What does he do, is your brother joong? Does he have business here?

L: Thats him, he is business man, he was based in LA, but now he is south
america, so I help him out when he is not here.

S: He brought large amount of cash and deposited to your account at the
beginning of the year, where did he get that money, and why did he give
you that amount?

L: Well, I was a student, and I pay 50k a year for my education, he helps me
with the tuition, so my parents and him bring me money.

S: This is not the first time, and you have also deposited 60k in 2008 , can
you confirm his port of the entry? Did he declare that money?

L: I think it was new york, and yes we declare everytime we bring in the cash.

S: So, your family is giving you money for school, what kind of business is
your brother involved in?

L: He does things related to computer parts, routers and stuff, don't really know technicalities. But he imports from china to brazil, and paraguay.
S: Then why is he using you as a middle man?
L: You shoudl know this, but international wires from south america to China can take upto two weeks, whereas receiving money to us account, and wiring back could be done in lest than two days.
S: I don't know any of that. But if you declared everytime you grought the money, do you have receipt?
L: Hm, I don't think I have any, I gave the slip to the customs, don't you have access to that?
S: I'm pretty sure we can. Are you an american, what about your brother?
L: No I'm south Korean with student status, He is also Korean.
S: Do you pay taxes? Does your brother pay traxes?
L: I do whenever I have income, I'm pretty sure he did too.
S: Ok, here what we need, I will give you my card, and you will mail me past two years of tax returns, and you will ask samething from your brother.
L: what happens, if he only did it back in brazil? do you still want that?
S: I'm pretty sure we have somebody who can look into that.
L: Can you write that down, and how soon you need the papers?
S: Let's say few weeks from now, does that work for you?
L: What is going on, Am I in trouble?
S: Well, we will give those papers to DAs office and they will decide. You said you were a painter, what is your plan?
L: Well am working on new projects and I have a show coming up...
S: well you've got a Yale MFA why don't you just paint?

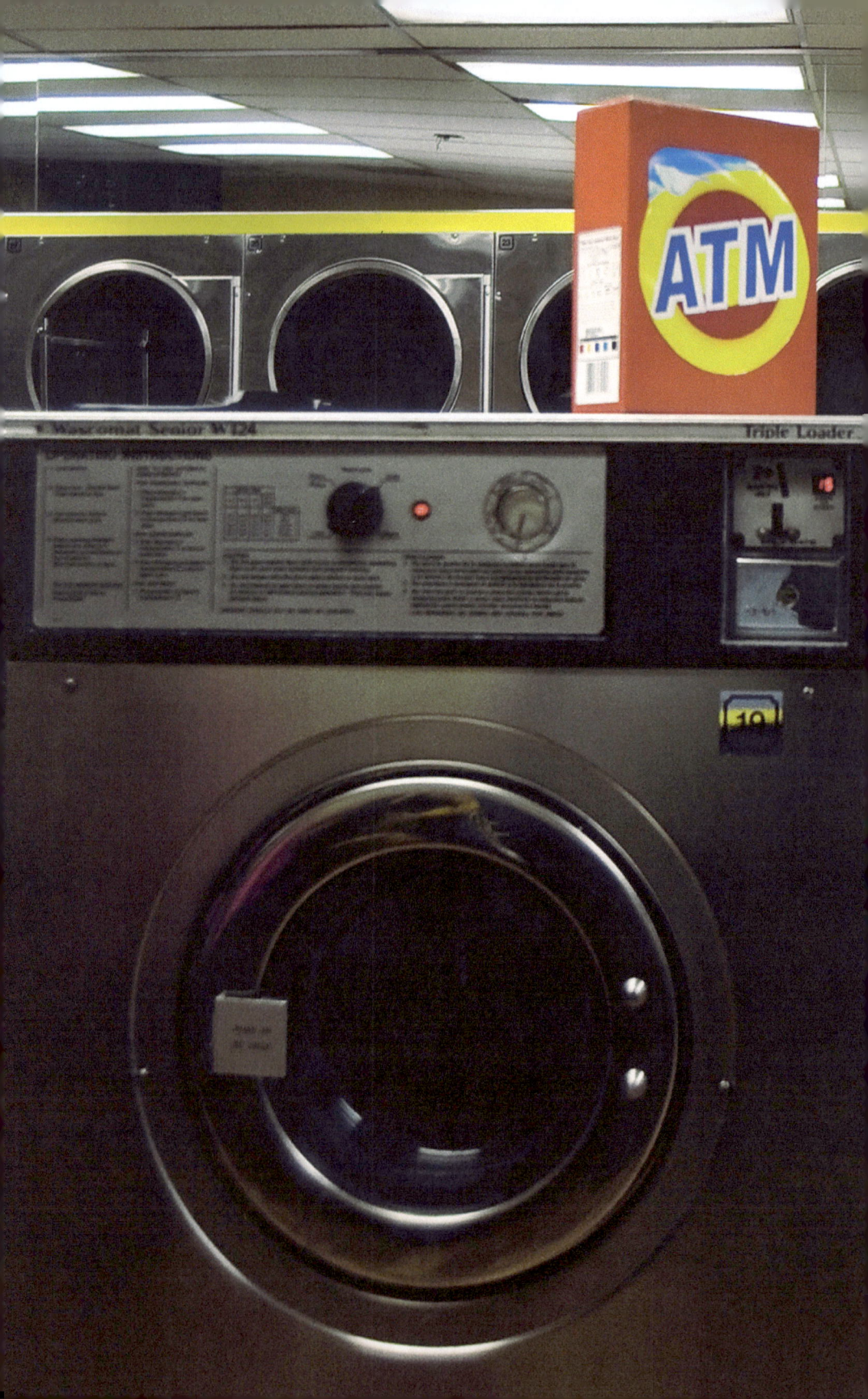

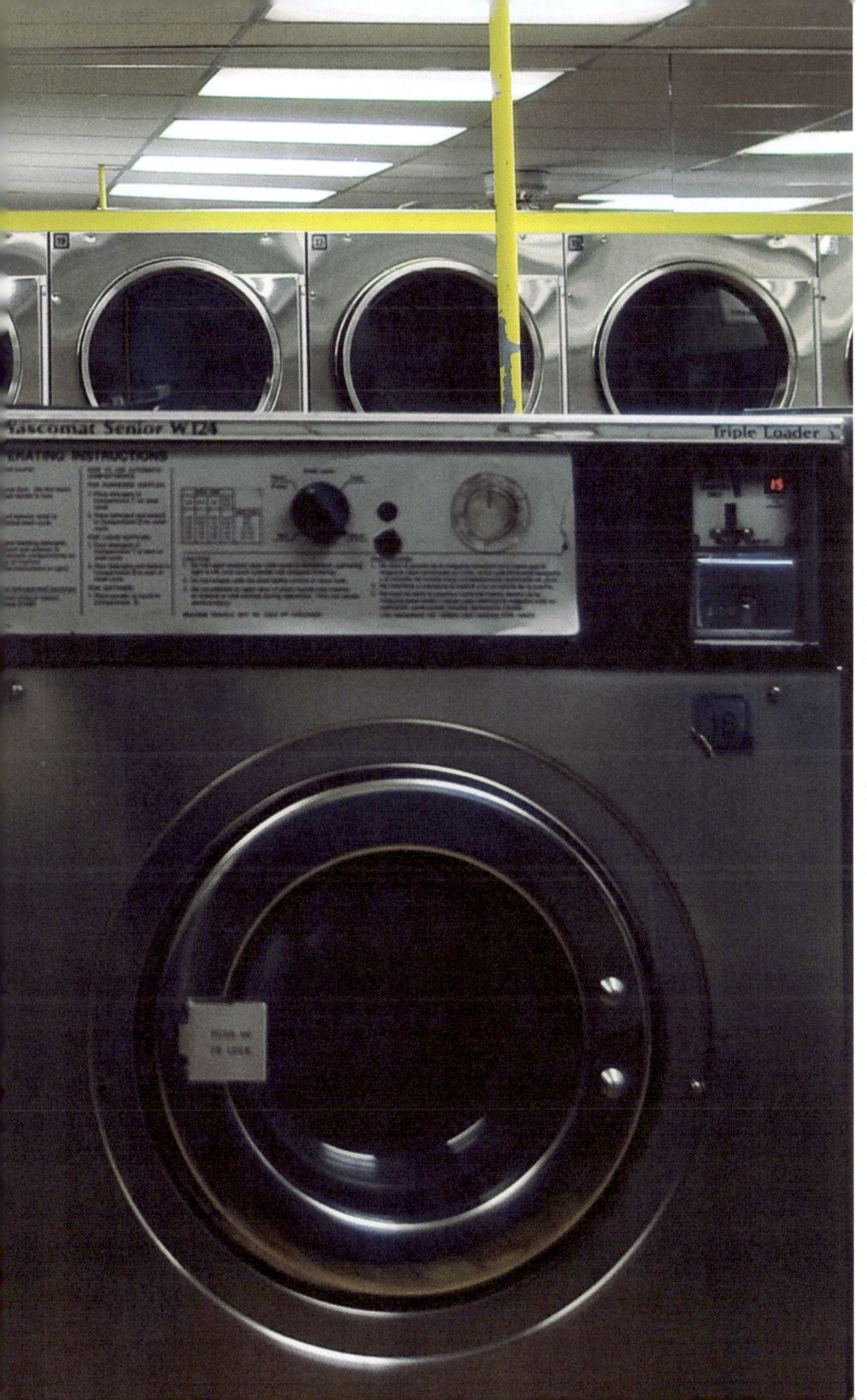

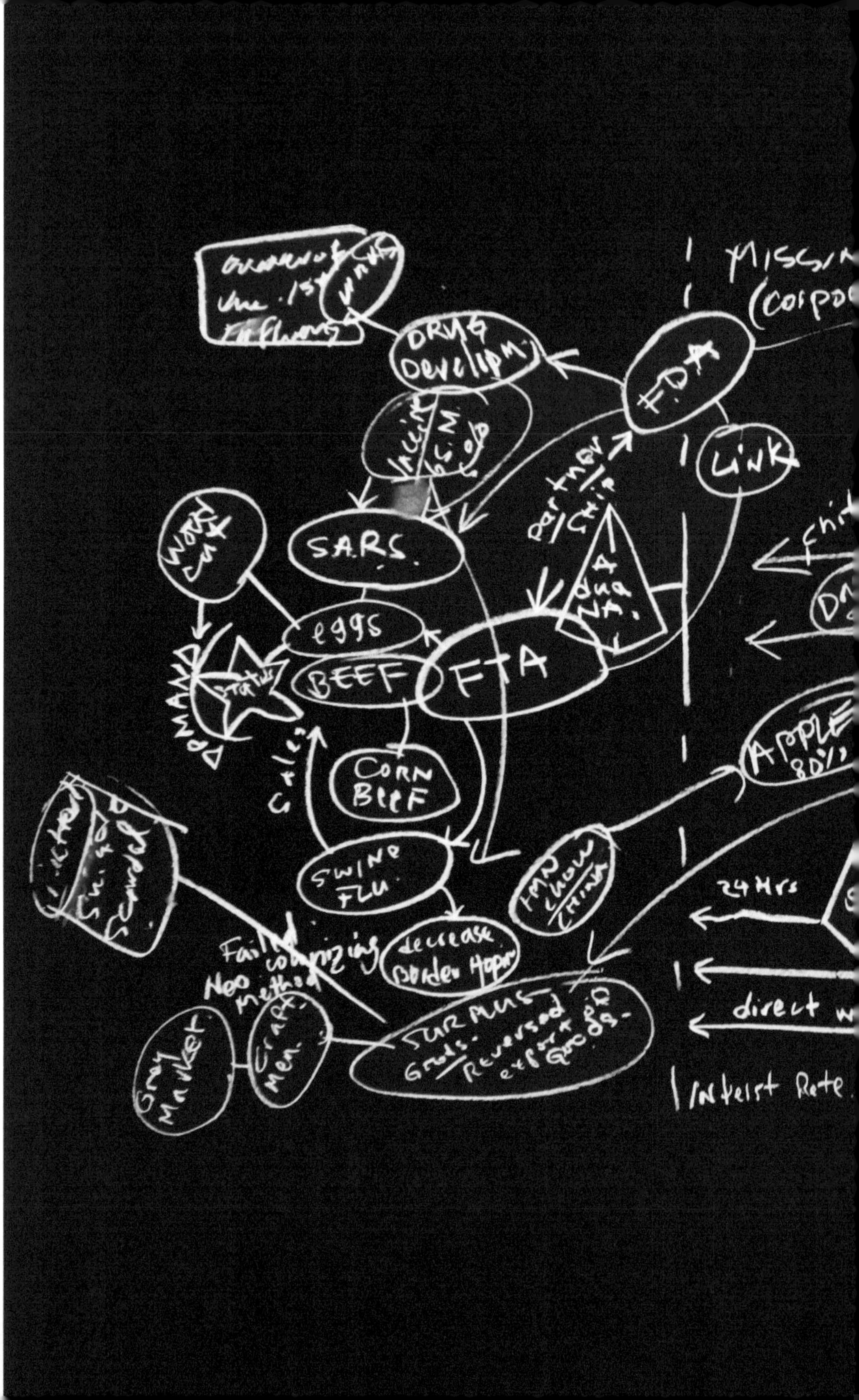
DRUG Developm
FDA
LINK
S.A.R.S.
eggs
BEEF
FTA
CORN BEEF
SWINE FLU
DEMAND
STATUS
Sales
decrease border Hopp
SURPLUS Goods. Reversed export goods.
Gray Market
Craft Men.
Failed Neo colonizing method
24 Hrs
direct w
Interest Rate.

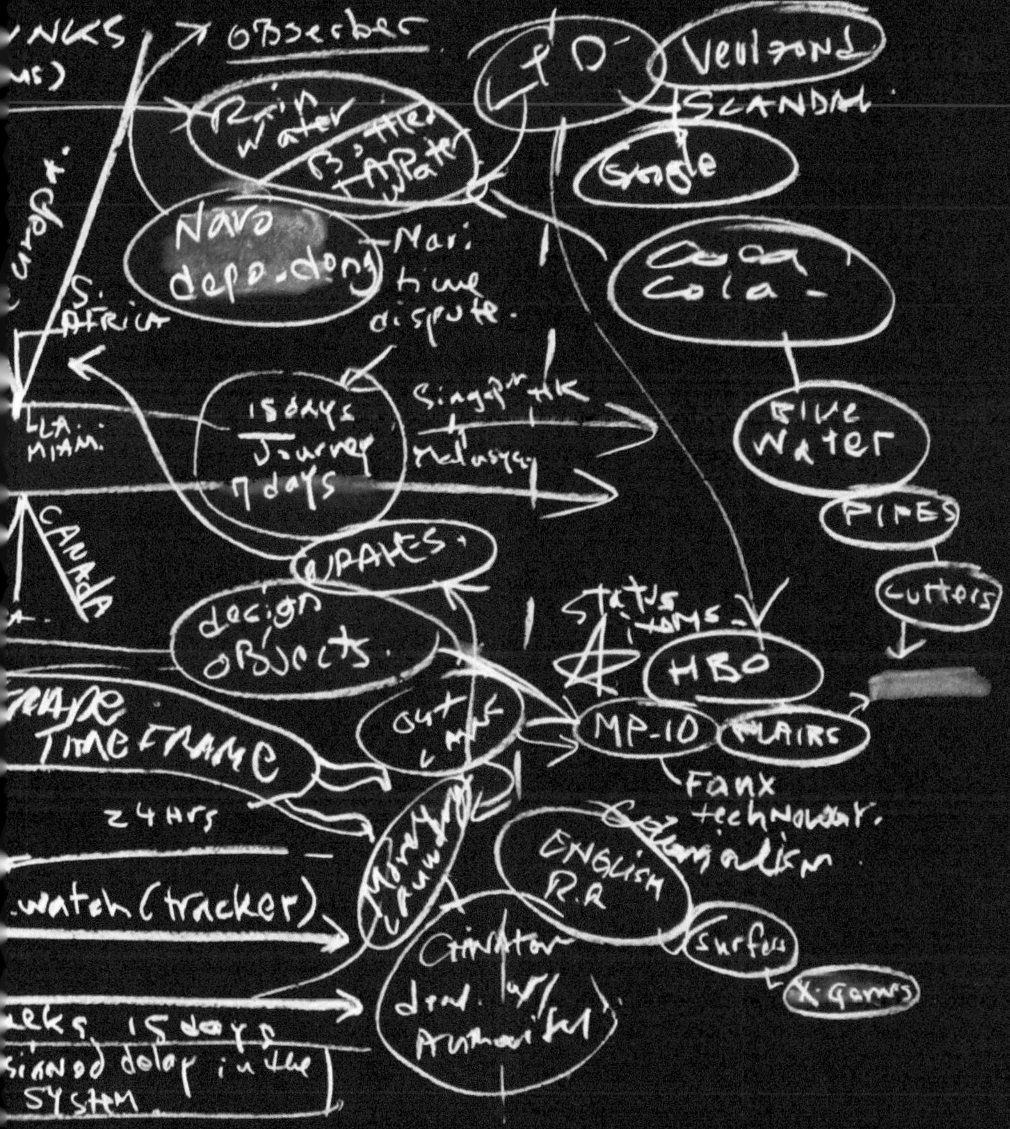

NKS → Observer
MS)

Rain Water
B's their
Affair

Navo
depe-deng — Mari-
time
dispute.

(PD) — Veuland
SCANDAL
Eagle
Coca Cola —

Blue Water
PIPES
Cutters

S.
AFRICA

LA
MIAMI.

15 days
Journey
7 days

Singapore
+
Malaysia

CANADA

RAMES.
design
OBJECTS.

STATUS
ITEMS —
HBO
MP-10   FLAIRS
Fanx
technolog.

TIMEFRAME

out
c man

colonialism

24 Hrs

ENGLISH
R.R
Surfers
X-Games

watch (tracker)

Aviator
dead w/
Animalist

eks 15 days
signed delay in the
SYSTEM.

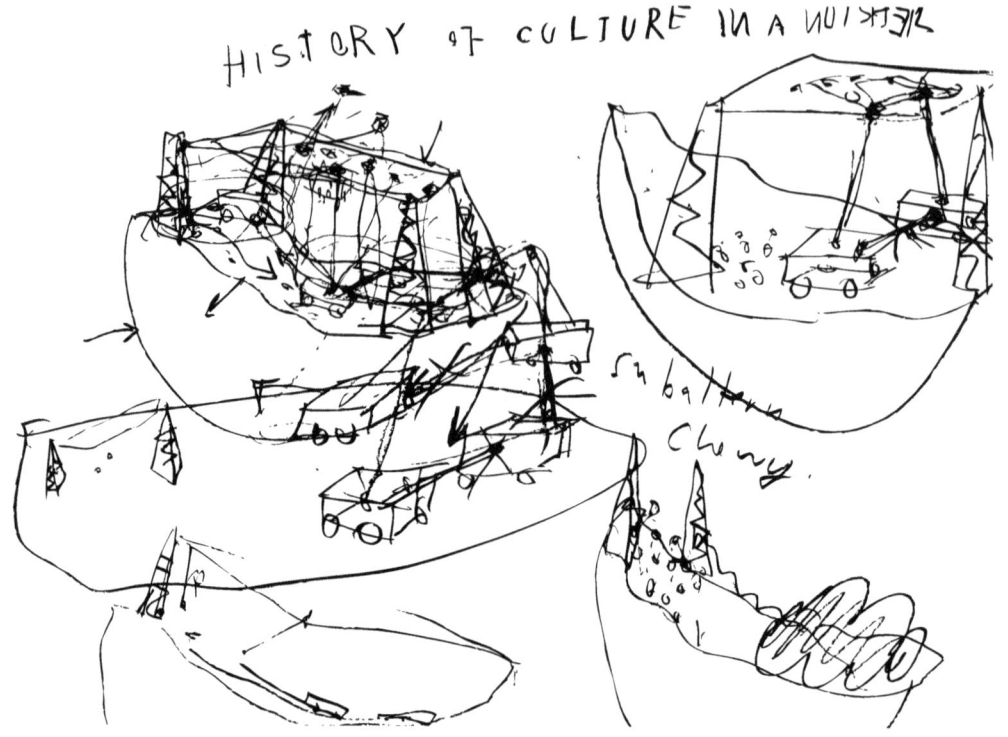

subaltern
Chung.

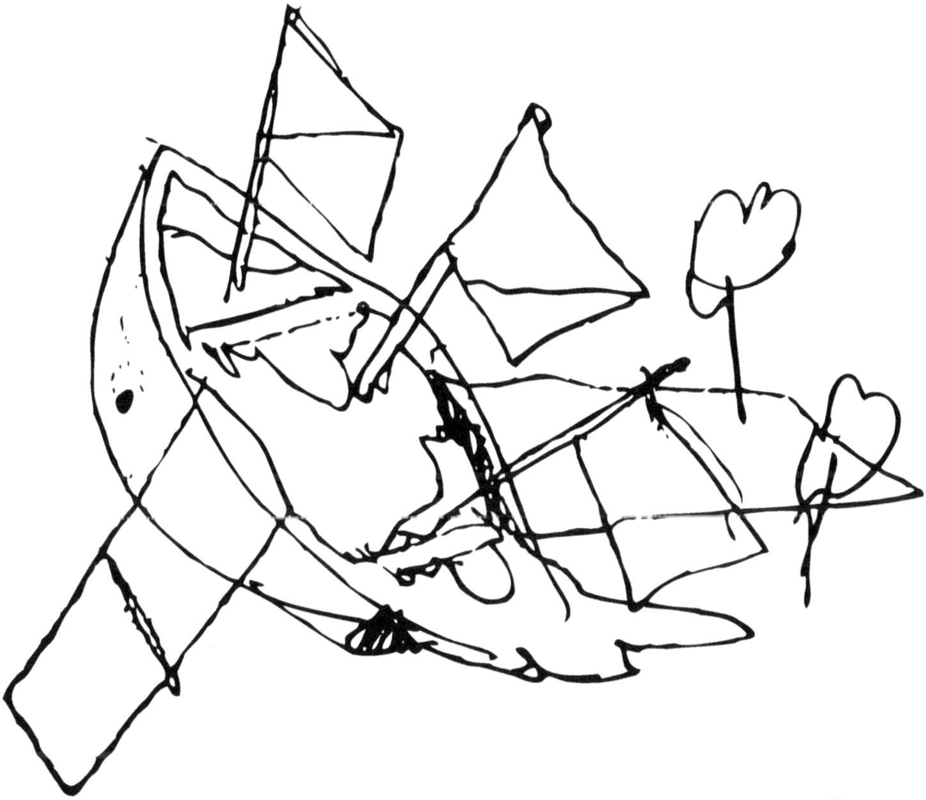

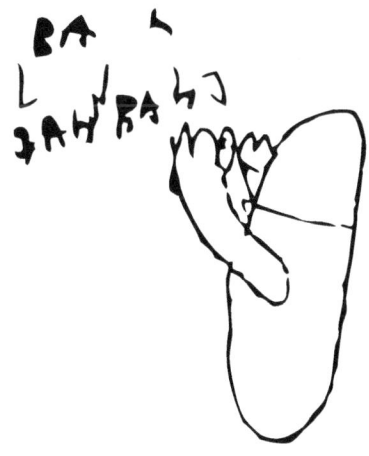

COMU

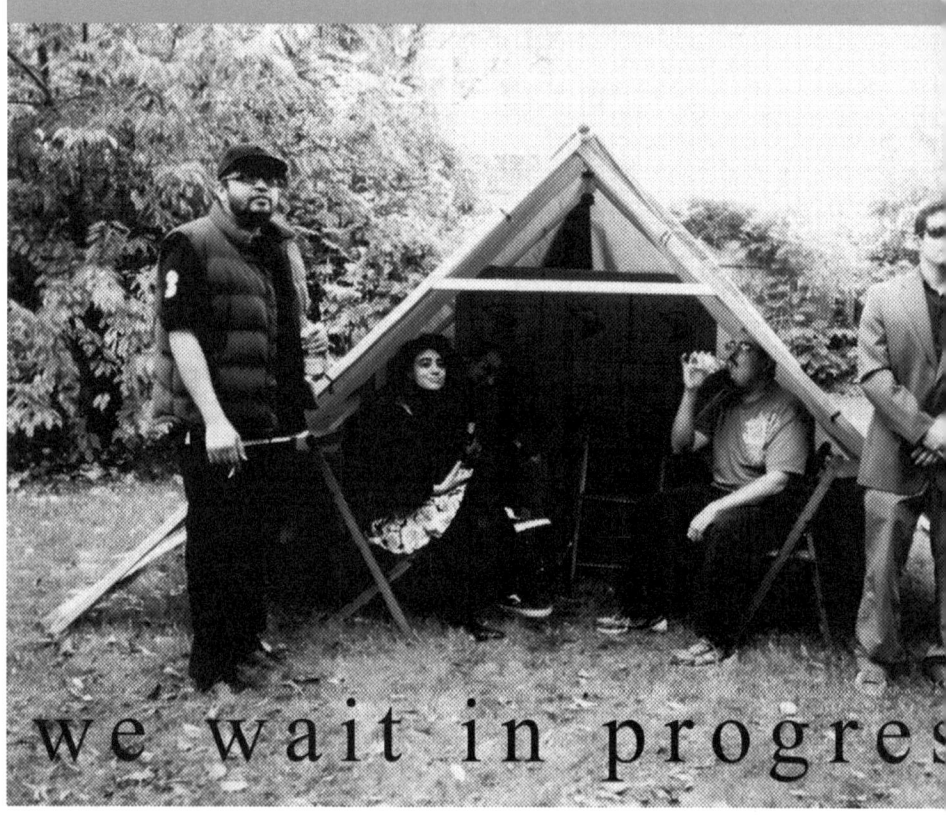

we wait in progres

A proposito: Pan Latino Dialoques

Reception: Sunday, October 25, 2-5pm, accompanying performance during the reception.
Linda Arredondo, Arthur Menezes Brum, Oscar Rene Cornejo, Abigail Deville, Manuela Gonzalez, Cheon Pyo Lee, Clynton Lowry, Troy Michi
Abel Rodriguez, and Edgar Serrano

Featuring works from 12 Yale MFA artists, A proposito: Pan-Latino Dialogues questions the boundaries and assumptions between identity and
a range of artistic approaches featuring paintings, sculptures, printmaking, installations and performances. Utilizing the architectural space
Gallery, the artists have assembled their works into a specially considered exhibition space to create an investigative dialogue between the ne
and a "latino style" or convention. Each work invents an aesthetic which is fruitful and pragmatic for dealing with contemporary issues. The v
expected to rest on prior definitions but hopes to expand our idea of what constitutes the art from a demographic. Instead, it is the desire of th
to the work with fresh eyes and a curiosity.
The ethnonym Latino has been both useful and uncomfortable for a group of people unbound by race whose political histories, traditions, reli
depart. It is an identity, whose foundation is hybridity, whose most profound characteristics have developed though syncretism and hetero-
accompany this definition as there are many, who with good reason bristle at its convenience, inaccuracy and generic proximity. The ethnony
dialogues which are individual and collective from varying commonalities and confluences of experience. As challengers, investigators, and
uncertainty, artists in this exhibition embrace qualities of both the provincial and the cosmopolitan by seeking a route between these tensions

John Slade Ely House, 51 Trumbull Street New Haven, CT 06510
Hours
Wednesday - Friday, 11am - 4pm

ICADO

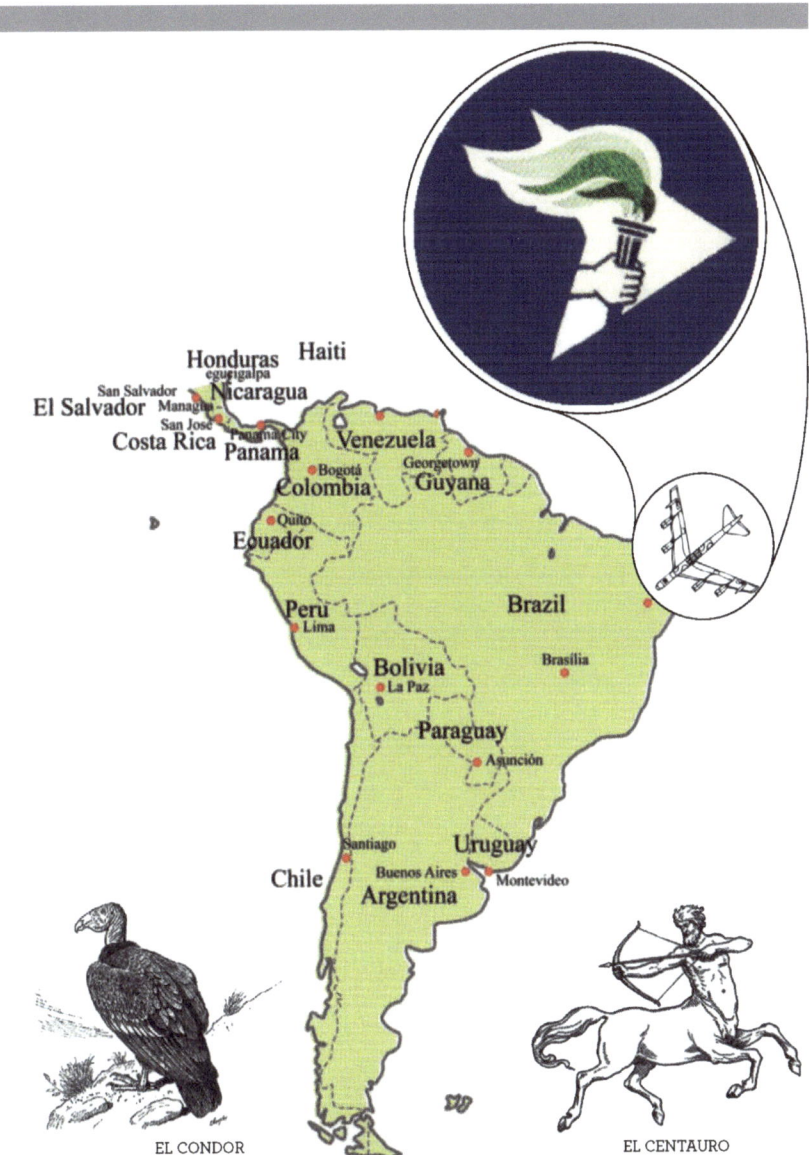

eana Ortega,

n showcases
e Ely House
ptive identity
show are not
viewers come

overlap and
n and doubt
ientation for
nalogue and

EL CONDOR   EL CENTAURO

La tierra quema

A proposito: Pan Latino Dialoques

Reception: Sunday, October 25, 2-5pm, accompanying performance during the reception.
Linda Arredondo, Arthur Menezes Brum, Oscar Rene Cornejo, Abigail Deville, Manuela Gonzalez, Cheon Pyo Lee, Clynton Lowry, Troy M.
Abel Rodriguez, and Edgar Serrano

Featuring works from 12 Yale MFA artists, A proposito: Pan-Latino Dialogues questions the boundaries and assumptions between identity a
a range of artistic approaches featuring paintings, sculptures, printmaking, installations and performances. Utilizing the architectural sp
Gallery, the artists have assembled their works into a specially considered exhibition space to create an investigative dialogue between the
and a "latino style" or convention. Each work invents an aesthetic which is fruitful and pragmatic for dealing with contemporary issues. T
expected to rest on prior definitions but hopes to expand our idea of what constitutes the art from a demographic. Instead, it is the desire o
to the work with fresh eyes and a curiosity.
The ethnonym Latino has been both useful and uncomfortable for a group of people unbound by race whose political histories, traditions, a
depart. It is an identity, whose foundation is hybridity, whose most profound characteristics have developed though syncretism and het
accompany this definition as there are many, who with good reason bristle at its convenience, inaccuracy and generic proximity. The ethno
dialogues which are individual and collective from varying commonalities and confluences of experience. As challengers, investigators,
uncertainty, artists in this exhibition embrace qualities of both the provincial and the cosmopolitan by seeking a route between these tensi

John Slade Ely House, 51 Trumbull Street New Haven, CT 06510
Hours
Wednesday - Friday, 11am - 4pm
Saturday & Sunday, 2pm - 5pm
(203) 624-8055
Free and Open to the Public

Alliance for Progress

Alliance for Progress, Span. Alianza para el Progreso, U.S. assistance program for Latin America begun in 1961 during the presidency of John F. Kennedy. It was created principally to counter the appeal of revolutionary politics, such as those adopted in Cuba (see Fidel Castro). It called for vast multilateral programs to relieve the continent's poverty and social inequities and ultimately included U.S. programs of military and police assistance to counter Communist subversion. The charter of the alliance, formulated at an inter-American conference at Punta del Este, Uruguay, in Aug., 1961, called for an annual increase of 2.5% in per capita income, the establishment of democratic governments, more equitable income distribution, land reform, and economic and social planning. Latin American countries (excluding Cuba) pledged a capital investment of $80 billion over 10 years. The United States agreed to supply or guarantee $20 billion. By the late 1960s, however, the United States had become preoccupied with the Vietnam War, and commitments to Latin America were reduced. Moreover, most Latin American nations were unwilling to implement needed reforms. The Organization of American States disbanded the permanent committee created to implement the alliance in 1973.

See A. F. Lowenthal, ed., Exporting Democracy: The United States and Latin America (1991)

Alliance Goes Global

Alliance for progress provides milk for Women and Children Refugees at The Hmong of Northeast Laos The Land and the People Camp.

Photograph by Paul E. White

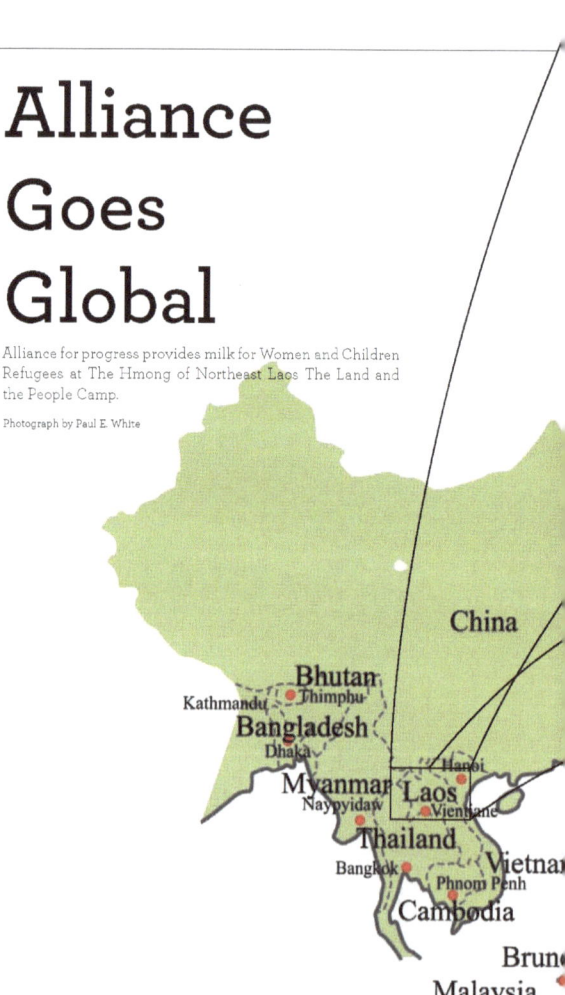

China

Bhutan
Thimphu
Kathmandu
Bangladesh
Dhaka
Hanoi
Myanmar Laos
Naypyidaw Vientiane
Thailand
Bangkok Vietna
Phnom Penh
Cambodia
Brun
Malaysia

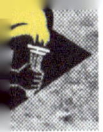

leana Ortega,

on showcases
de Ely House
ptive identity
show are not
viewers come

es overlap and
on and doubt
orientation for
analogue and

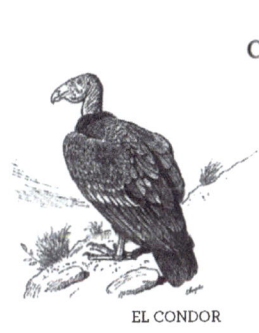
EL CONDOR

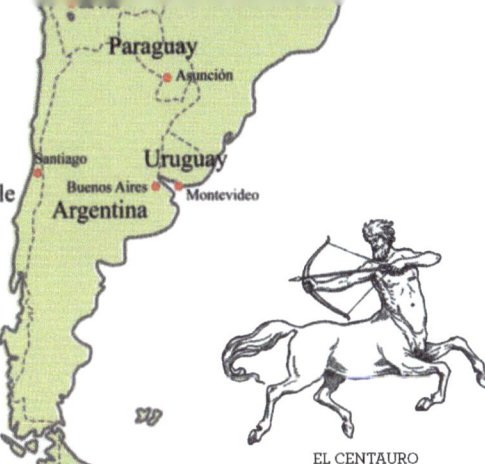

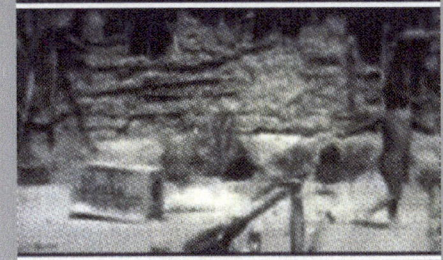
EL CENTAURO

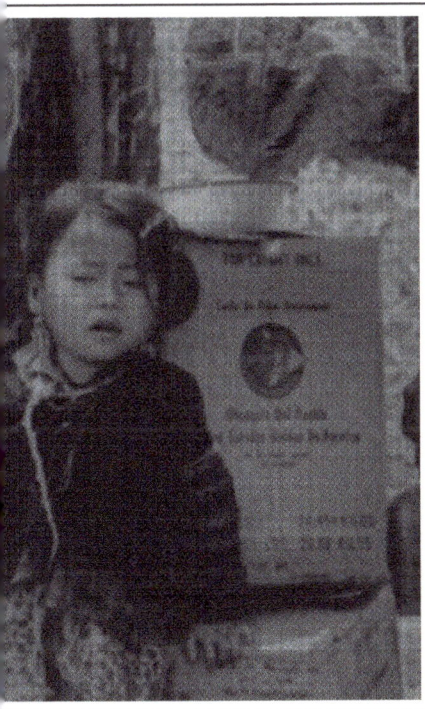

La tierra quema

Writer/director/producer, Raymundo Gleyzer (12 min.)
In The land burns, Raymundo Gleyzer exposes the inequities of
land ownership in Brazil.
During her visit to Yale Raymundo's window Juane Sapire,
remembers how he found out about empty 'Alliance for progress"
that were dropped in Northern region of the Brazil. On Thursday,
May 27, 1976, Raymundo Gleyzer disappeared in Buenos Aires.
He had been kidnapped by the military. In response to inquiries
from 20 U.S. senators, the CIA said that he had harbored Chilean
refugees – fleeing the government of Augusto Pinochet – in his
home. No one ever saw Gleyzer again.
He was 34 years old.

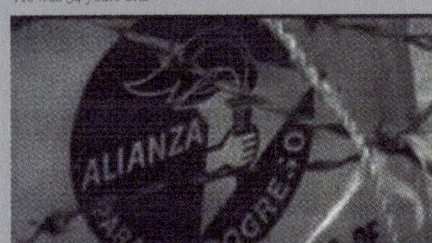

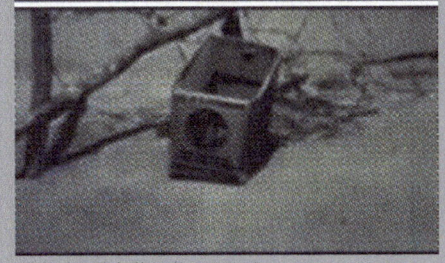

Still Shots from "The land burns / La tierra quema"

egawan

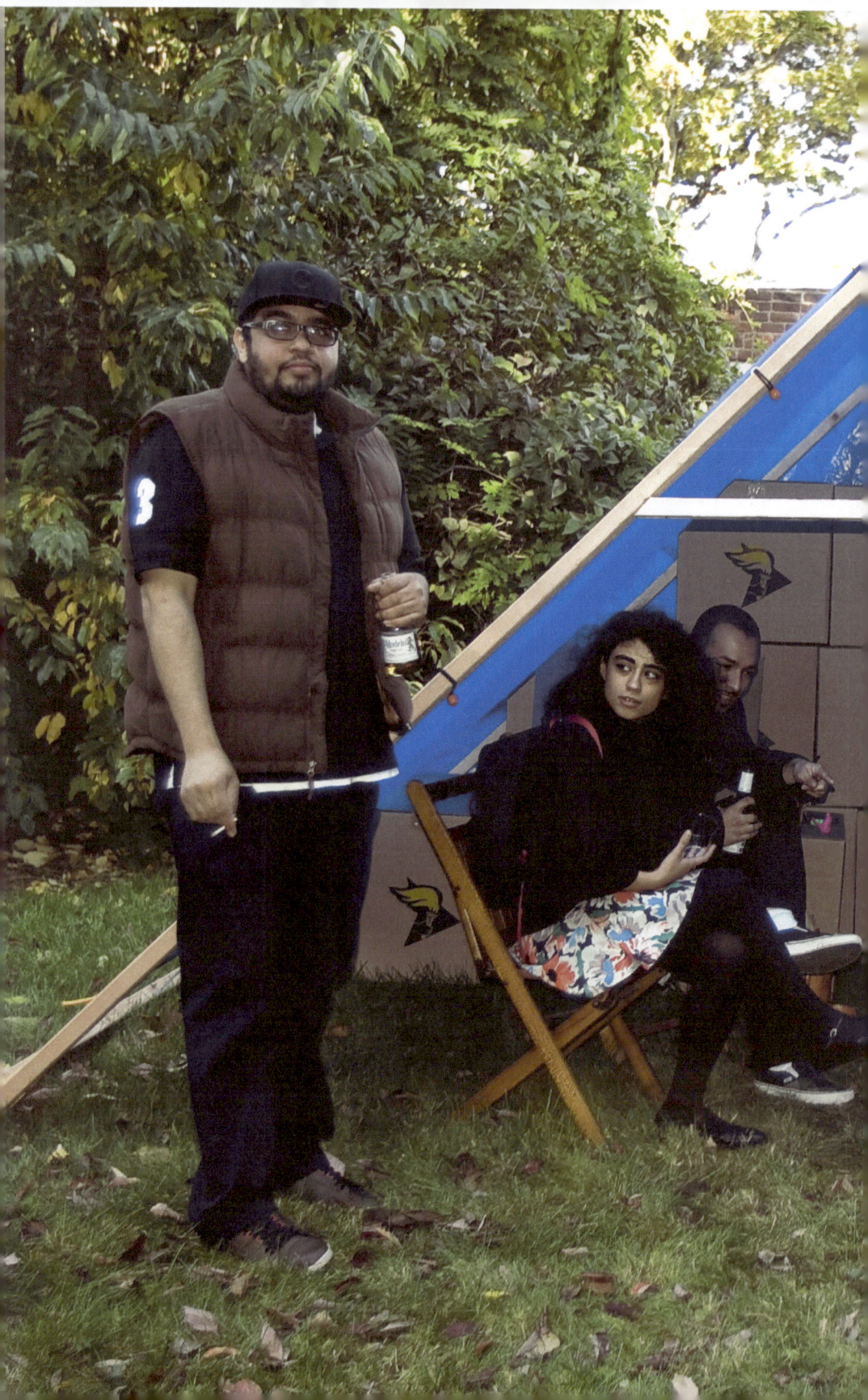

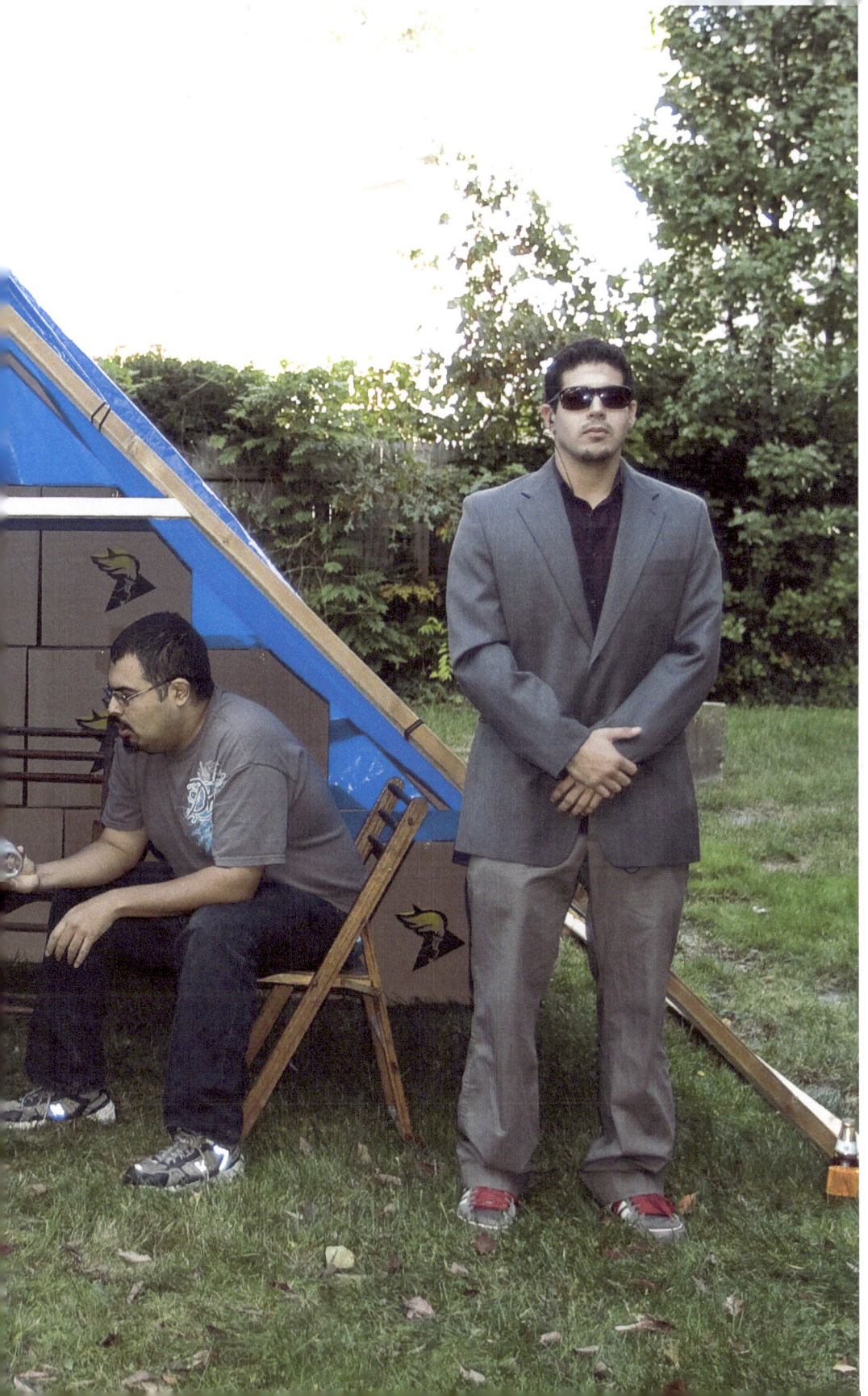

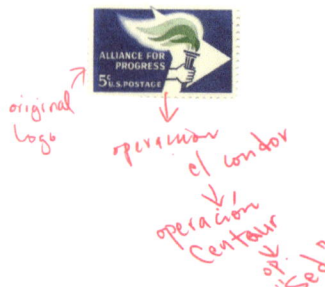

original logo

operacion el condor

operación Centaur

op "Sede"

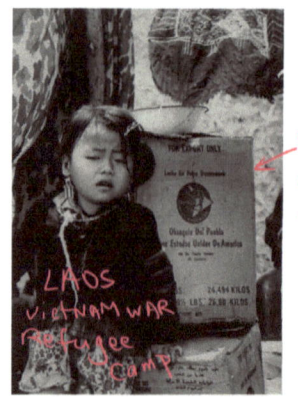

Surplus supplies recycled.

LAOS VIETNAM WAR refugee camp

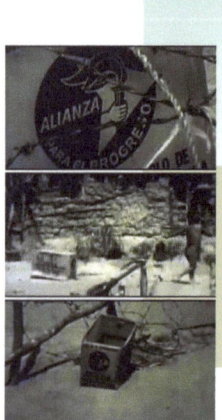

The land burns, Argentina, 1963. D. Raymundo Gleyzer

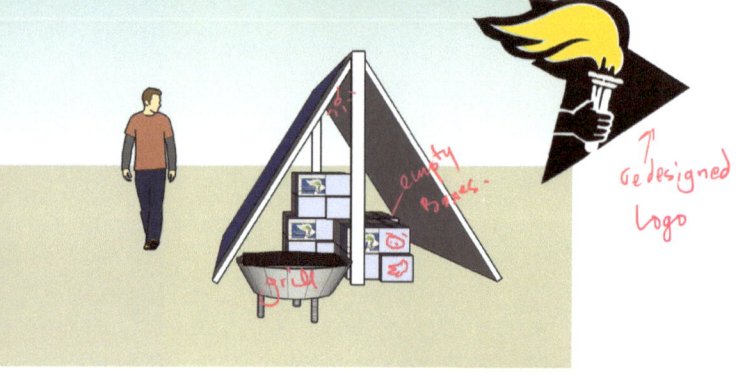

grill

empty boxes.

redesigned logo

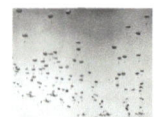

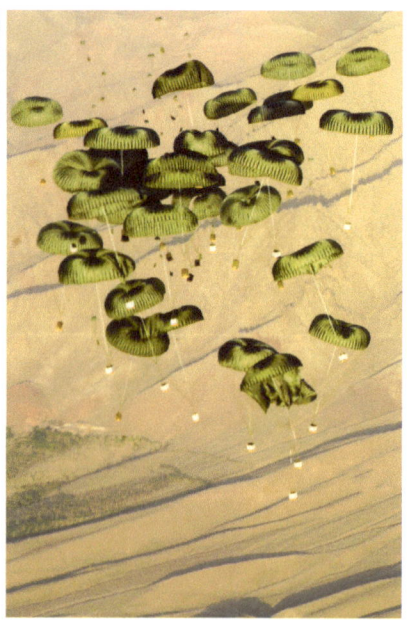

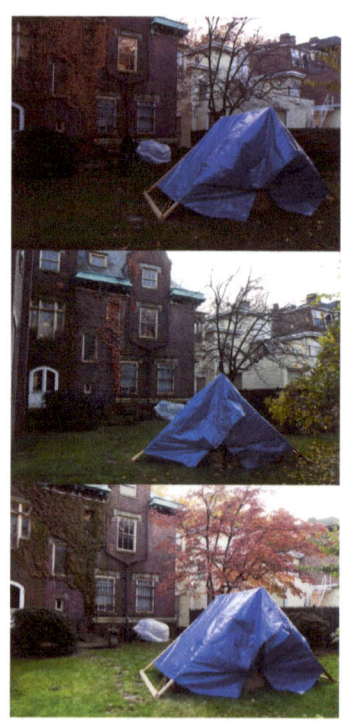

Easy ideas and fearful future imagined.

God favors the bold/shameless
Comunicados, Omleggs, MPX, 2009

Chinese business interests were combining real and fake in the same
packages to slake the appetite of desperate consumers. So I fashioned my
own eggs (from wood), along with their unique packaging, and worked
with genetic engineers to devise better. We imagined our prototype egg
would include sausage and bacon within its shell.

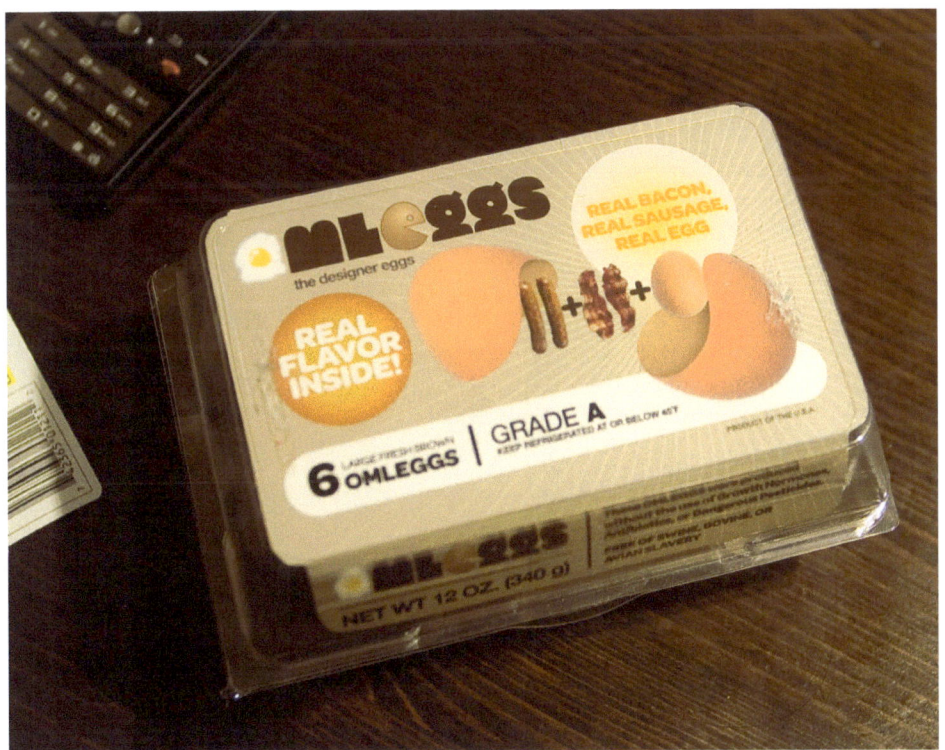

COMU

Scientists 'grow' meat in laboratory

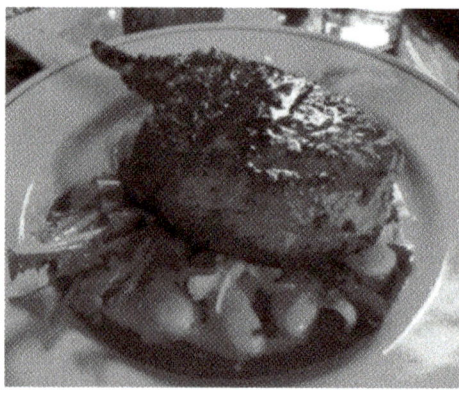

The move towards artificially engineered foods has taken a step forward after scientists grew a form of meat in a laboratory for the first time.

Scientists in the Netherlands have successfully synthesized some real-deal pork meat without having to kill any pigs. Sure, it's not quite edible yet, but they predict you'll be eating labmeat in a mere five years.

What they made this time is what they're calling "soggy pork," which is fake pig muscle that's pretty gross because it's never been exercised. But once they figure out how to tone it up in the lab, you'll be looking at guilt-free pork chops.

And it's amazing news, really. Not only will vegetarians get to enjoy the deliciousness that is meat without guilt, but it'll do wonders for the environment. Do you realize how horrible the beef industry is for ol' Mother Nature? Very, very horrible. If we could replace all those factory farmed animals with slabs of meat rolling off an assembly line, we'd be doing the planet and animals a whole lot of good.

That is, provided it tastes good. If it doesn't, no one will eat it, and this will all be for naught. So make sure it's succulent, scientists!

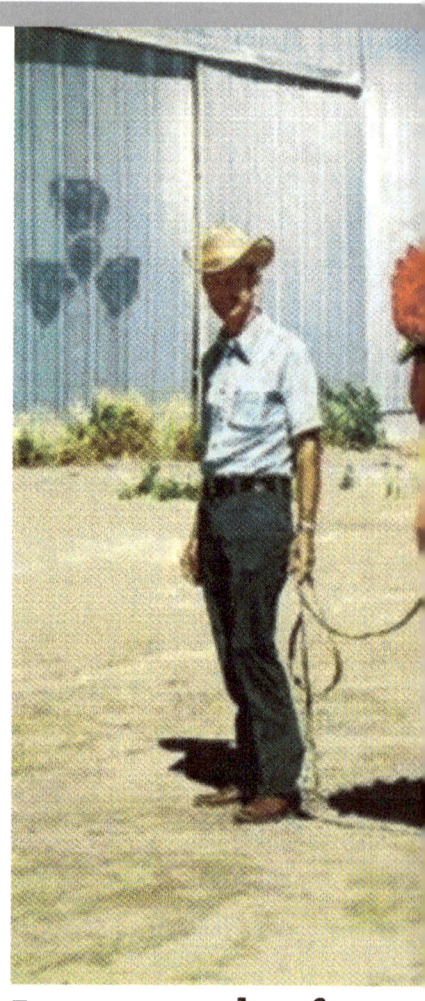

La morte ha fatto

Fast food, a dinner for four?

ICADO

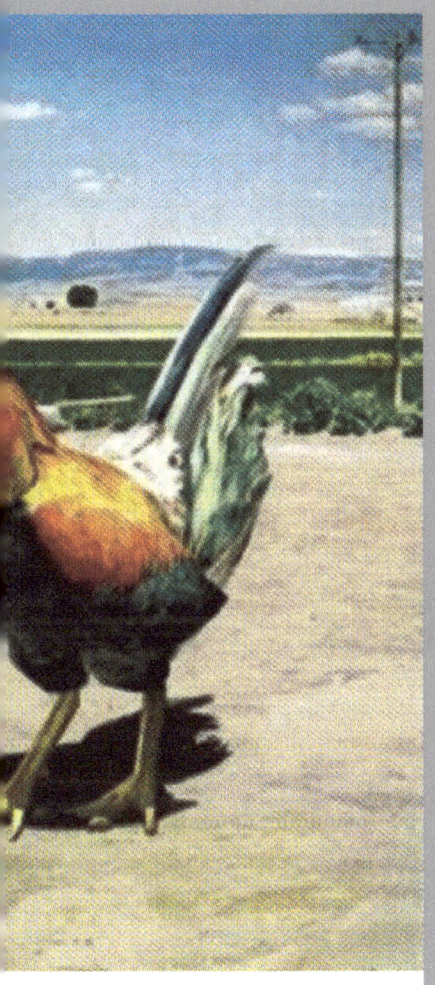

JO (1968)

n. It involves Anna (who owns the farm), her husband Marco
). Marco continues to kill as jealousy becomes more prevalent

Man-made Fake Eggs Sold on China Market

Posted by chinaview on August 15, 2007

Zhengzhou city's local newspaper Zhengzhou Daily (Zhengzhou is the capital city of Henan province, in Central China) reported on Aug 13, 2007 that resident Mr. Wang, who's selling food additive for many years, found that the chicken eggs he bought on night market didn't look natural. This experience in food told him the "eggs" were made by additive!

So he caught the boss of the restaurant and asked him to tell the truth, otherwise he will sue them to the authority. The boss then reluctantly told Ms. Wang that the eggs were totally man-made, he actually didn't make it himself but bought it from a producer, and had finally told him the process of how to make fake "eggs".

After put the "egg" inside a calcium carbonate eggshell, a complete egg is ready, it only takes less than 5 minutes.

Why make fake eggs?

Because of money.

The cost of fake egg is only 0.55 Yuan/kg, while the true eggs market price is 5.6 Yuan/kg.

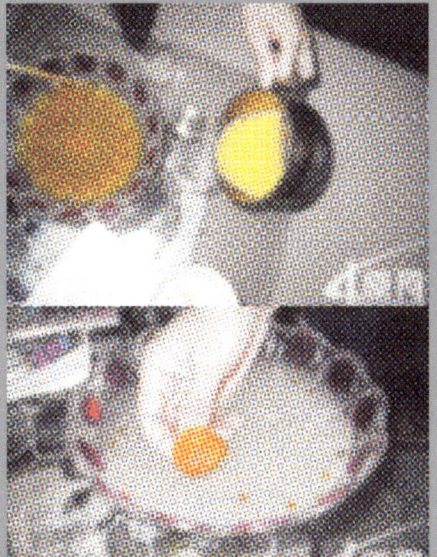

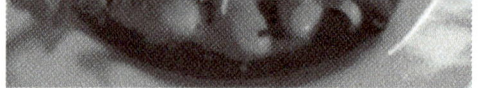

The move towards artificially engineered foods has taken a step forward after scientists grew a form of meat in a laboratory for the first time.

Scientists in the Netherlands have successfully synthesized some real-deal pork meat without having to kill any pigs. Sure, it's not quite edible yet, but they predict you'll be eating labmeat in a mere five years.

What they made this time is what they're calling "soggy pork," which is fake pig muscle that's pretty gross because it's never been exercised. But once they figure out how to tone it up in the lab, you'll be looking at guilt-free pork chops.

And it's amazing news, really. Not only will vegetarians get to enjoy the deliciousness that is meat without guilt, but it'll do wonders for the environment. Do you realize how horrible the beef industry is for ol' Mother Nature? Very, very horrible. If we could replace all those factory farmed animals with slabs of meat rolling off an assembly line, we'd be doing the planet and animals a whole lot of good.

That is, provided it tastes good. If it doesn't, no one will eat it, and this will all be for naught. So make sure it's succulent, scientists!

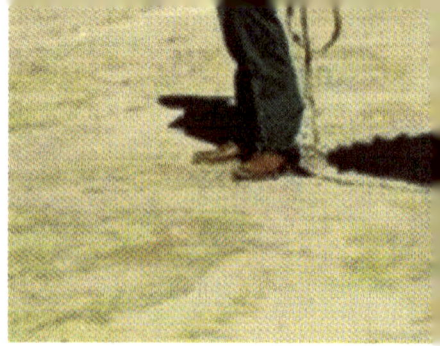

La morte ha fatto

A love triangle develops between three people who run a high te (who kills prostitutes in his spare time) and Gabriella (the very be on the farm.

Fast food, a dinner for four?

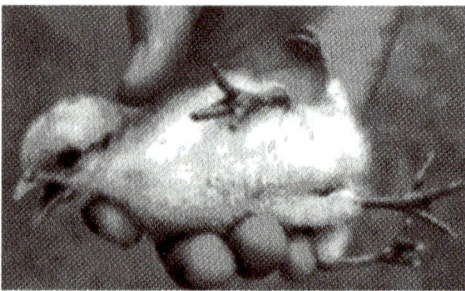

London-Terry O'Connell is a man on a mission, the thirty six year old farmer from Essex has just unveiled the first of his genetically engineered farm animals which he is hoping will soon grace the nation's dinner tables.

The bird pictured here is named Perhaps Colin and has been genetically manipulated to produce four tasty legs and so end the typical 'who gets a leg' argument familiar to every family of four.

Speaking to me earlier by telephone from his one hundred acre Essex farm, Mr O'Connell told me how he came up with this revolution in chicken leg technology I originally developed the birds as racing animals and was intent on setting up a chicken racing circuit similar to the Formula one franchise, but the original backers dropped out due to the bird flu scare and I was left with six thousand four legged racing chickens.

"The breakthrough came when I was really getting desperate, I had spent the day trying to train my fastest chicken, Mottled Jim, to complete a specially designed steeplechase course I'd based on the grand national course at Aintree.

Everything was going well until he came tearing down the course up to the Beecher's brook fence he then totally misjudged the height and came down hard on one of his back legs.

I don't mind telling you, I was in floods of tears when I realized his racing career was over.

It was my wife who suggested we should eat him as a tribute to a career unfulfilled.

It was then during Mottled Jim's tribute dinner that I suddenly realized each one of the four people at the table were chewing on one of Mottled Jim's legs, it was my eureka moment.'

Since his eureka moment Mr O'Connell has secured two lucrative supermarket contracts and is in talks with a certain fast food company whom he refuses to name at this present time but did reveal they were very interested in coating some of Mr O'Connell's former athletes in secret spices and seeing how it goes.

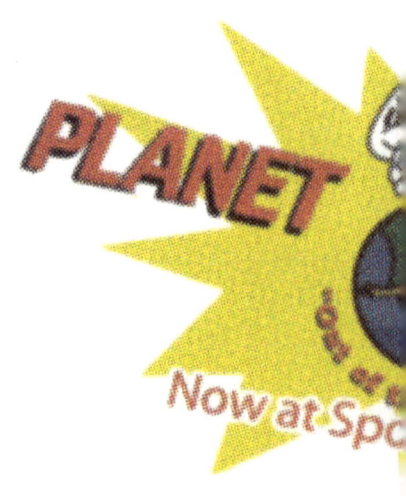

Growing Organs on Hosts

Scientists in Israel have grown perfect miniature human and pig kidneys inside mice whose immune systems are deficient. They took small clumps of cells from embryos 6-8 weeks old and implanted them into the mice. If pigs had been used, the resulting kidneys would have been normal size and could possibly have been used in transplantation. The work raises huge ethical problems. For example, most people would think it morally wrong to clone someone, implant the cloned embryo into a mother's womb, and then abort it in order to get hold of primitive tissues which are then grown in an immune deficient animal.

- Nature Medicine. DOI. 10.1038/nm812. December 2002

Oscar M
one-of-a-

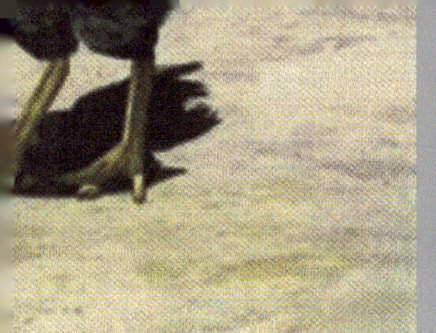

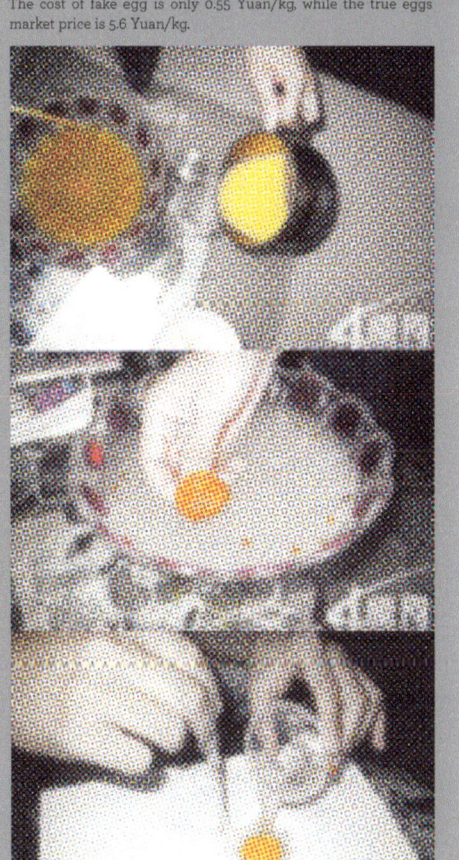

O (1968)

It involves Anna (who owns the farm), her husband Marco
Marco continues to kill as jealousy becomes more prevalent

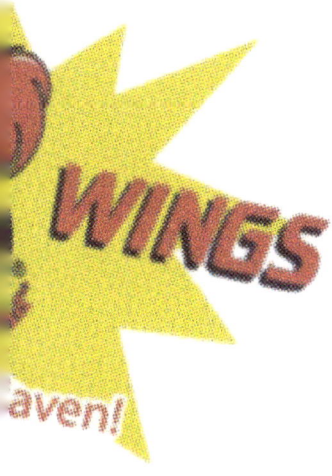

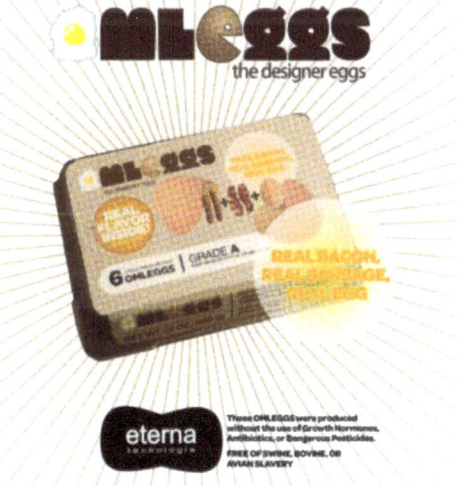

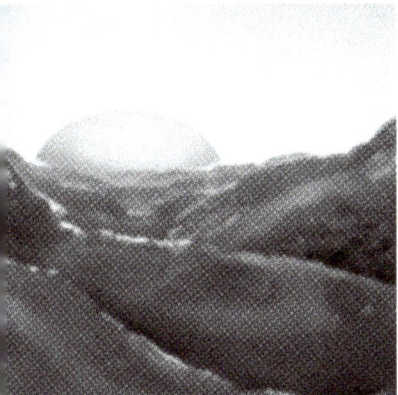

selected, hand-trimmed and naturally hardwood smoked for hours to bring you that
waking up for.

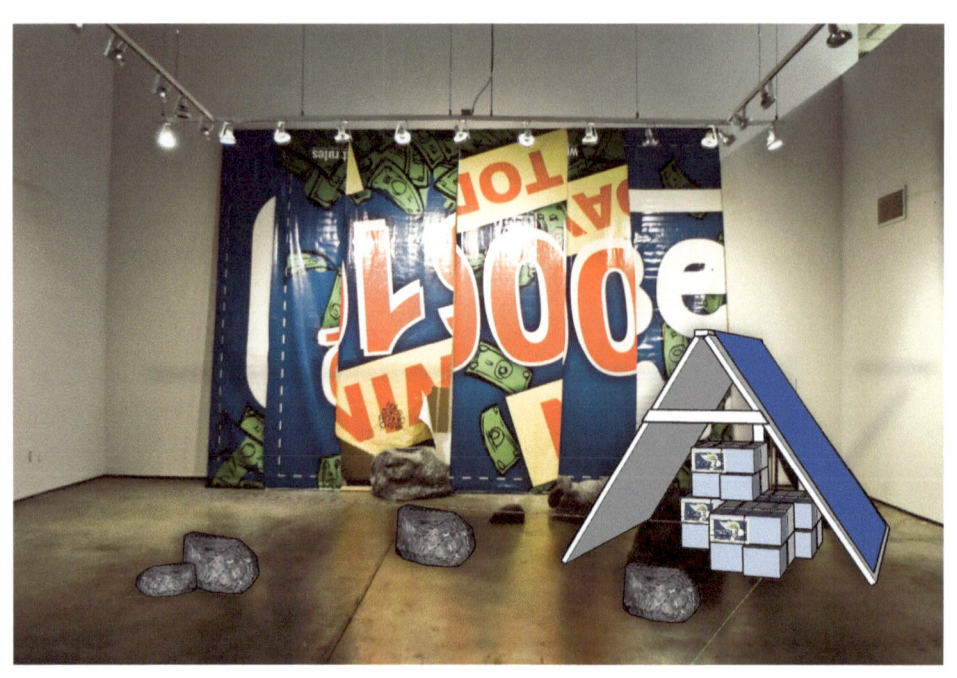

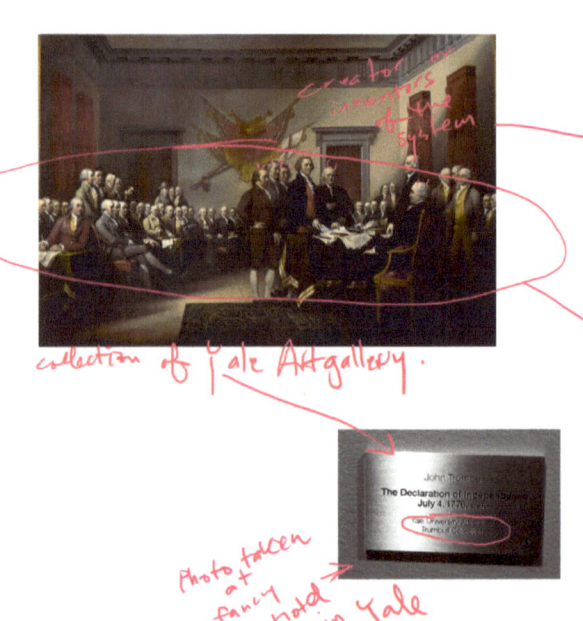

collection of Yale Artgallery.

John Trumbull
The Declaration of Independence
July 4, 1776

Photo taken
at
fancy hotel in Yale

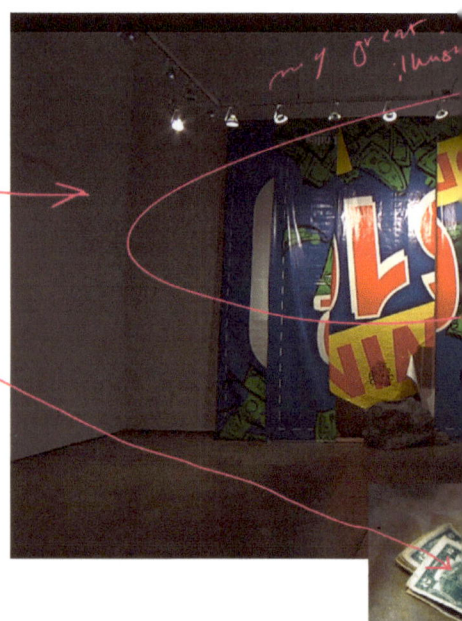

my great illus...

lucky from my

Who owns the technology?
And how is it all the bad people are actually
pushing culture foward.
Lawsuits and patenting the sun/iphone
Make do technology- Luis vitton pattern maker.

Small manufacturers in china were launching
products named mp4, mp5, mp7.
product naming has no connection to MPEG-1
Audio Layer 3.

Incrementing number is based on functions
that makers were adding in. I decided to create
an ultimate MP machine, a MPX.
Added functions that are not street legal forced
it to stay only as a prototype.

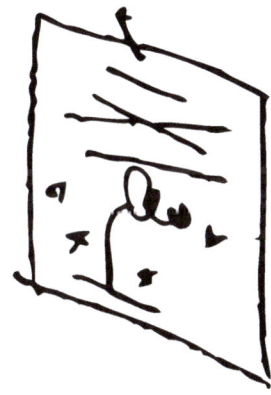

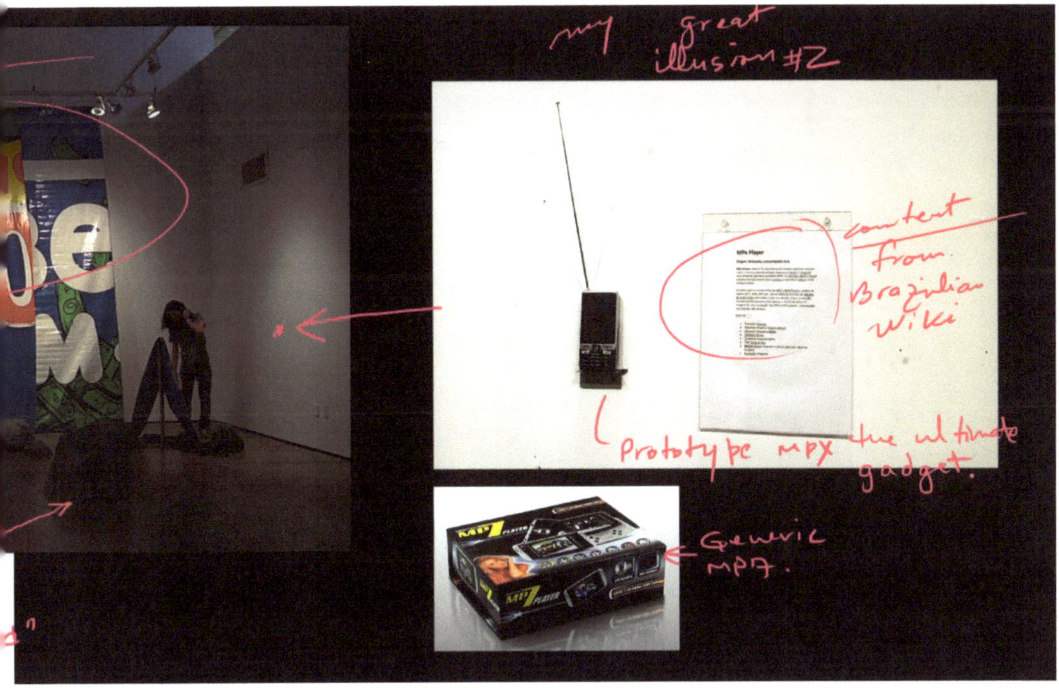

Collaboration with my brothers who happens to be IMPORT EXPORT EXPERTS!

My goal was to learn about economy and consequences of action, while creating temporary economy, (or shift of value for very brief time)

object no 1

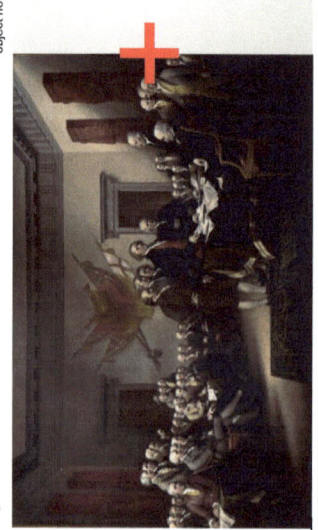

my father sends me two dollar bills as he thinks its good luck charm.

the initial interest was to trace the meaning of the painting in two dollar bills. "Trumbull's Declaration of Independence, family ties with yale, and reproduced in bank note as well as hotel lobby. (at the study)

+

object no 2

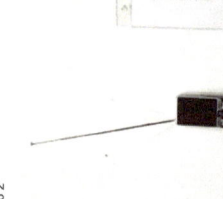 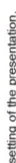

how is a hit product created?
what is the creation process for an objects aura?
(funtionality, design)

what is a process of derivation? MP3 <--> MPX
is this process logical?

small manufacturers in china were launching products named mp4, mp5, mp7, product naming has no connection to MPEG-1 Audio Layer 3. incrementing number is based on functions that makers were adding in.

I decided to create an ultimate MP machine, so I named my product MPX. adding functions that are not street legal. running into a problem of locking the functions before I could present it to the market. So, my mpx player only exists as a prototype.

=

setting of the presentation.

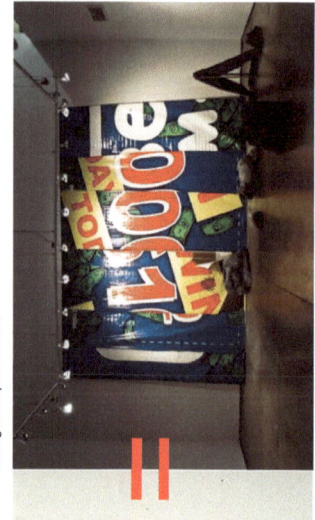

the backdrop for my presentation is a landscape painting made out of new haven lotto billboard sign. fake rocks were added to enhance the ambiance of tough market.

This was more theatrical, 'formal' component of the project.
the trumble replica was on left wall, and the mpx player was presented on right wall of the billboard.

tinued.

ideas continued.

Initial idea -bank wire stament- shipping time span.
re-routing and its consequences.uncovered routing ways. mapping the way of product, and payment

same actions different reactions,
imminent threat and its meaning.

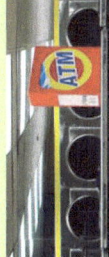

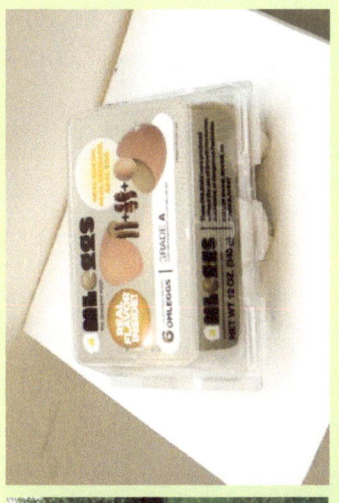

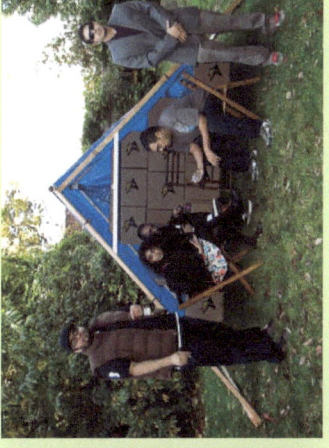

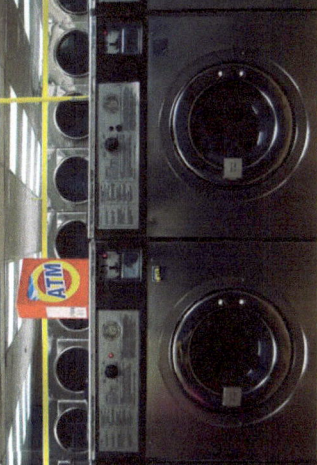

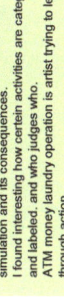

simulation and its consequences.
I found interesting how certain activities are categorized
and labeled. and who judges who.
ATM money laundry operation is artist trying to learn
through action.

Wait for progress.
'operations' was based on historical
operations done by us gov. towards S.
america. I was interested in the
consequences of such activities.

-wooden egg.
basic mechanis of retail shop, the real value of product. status item.

artists competiting/inspired by/with fradulant product.

all three projects are contingent on my interest on corporate, government relationship.
public = private entity.
Parts of the research, and results of each research were presented in a news paper format, labeled comunicados.
which is based on spanish word for offial press release form.

Design to fail, design to profit.
I have a 'erupting volcano' toy. It comes with a manual that has descriptions and image
of 'ring of fire', map of active volcanoes. Interestingly the map looks similar to the colonial
map drawn by English trade man. On the other hand a James bond movie "You Only Live
Twice" is another element as a space ship from of an erupting volcano is presented as a
menace to the modern world.

Like volcano and rockets, you have to exhaust /excess the anger to break free
or demolish your environment.

My plan is to produce toys that subvert the ideas embedded in the original. I am thinking
of a method to connect the technology and science kits as medium to tie the contingency
of technology to post colonialist endeavors.

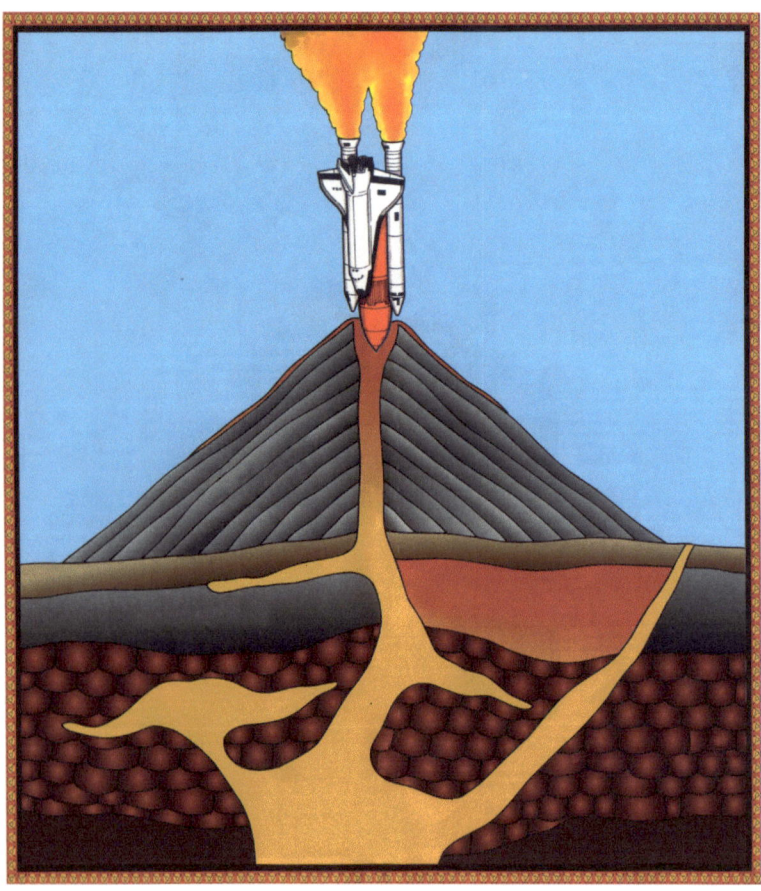

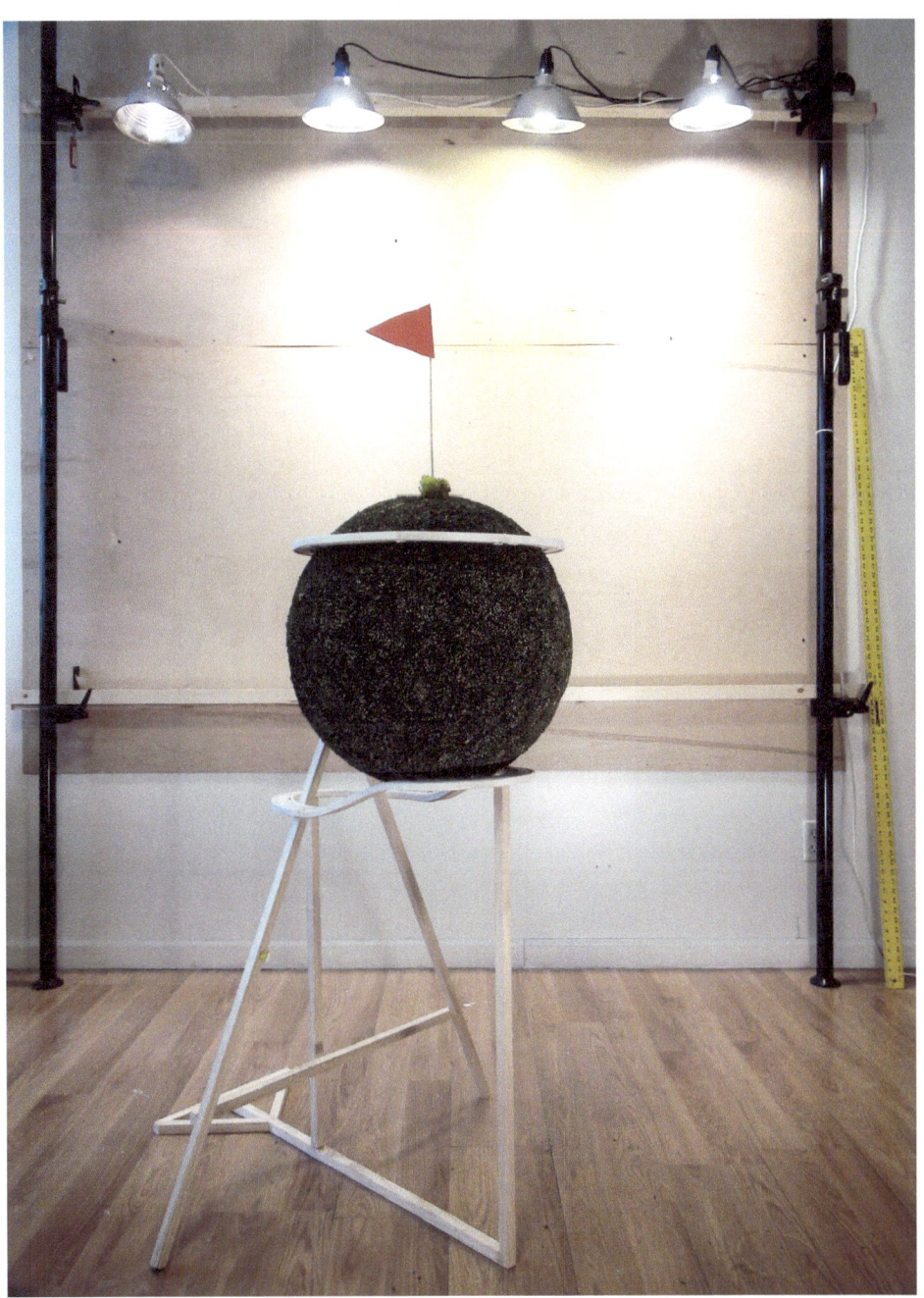

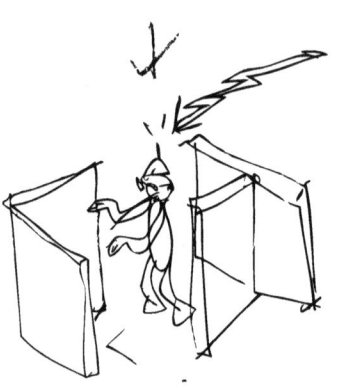

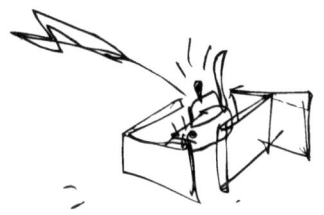

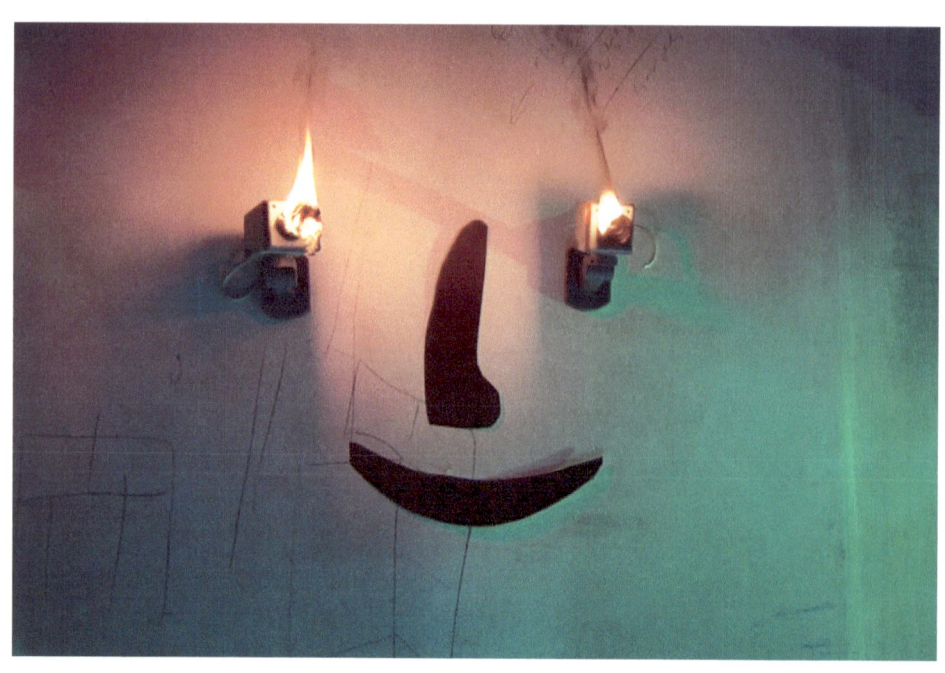

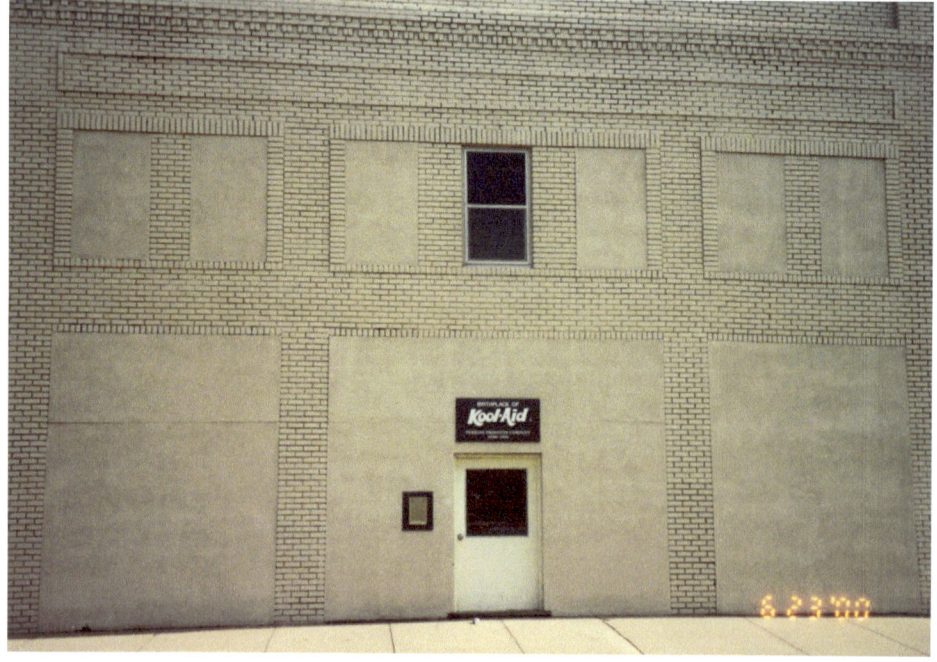

Toyota has to recall 600,000 of their vehicles, because of apparent danger of Prius and Lexus.

My friend Oscar is from El Salvador, he grew up seeing images of dead bodies in Toyota truck. The trucks reminds him of the horror.

Oscar likes Toyota trucks, but dislikes the memory. We walked around New Haven listening to Oscar explaining each truck's technical specification as well as how they can be used for transporting murder.

NGO and guerilla terrorists both use Toyota trucks.
Is the medium contingent to the user? What is the difference between memory and experience. It is simple and contradictory questions like Are you crying? Or are you sad? Advertisements and propaganda are dangerous, because it can not be avoided. Then what can one do in this uncontrollable state?

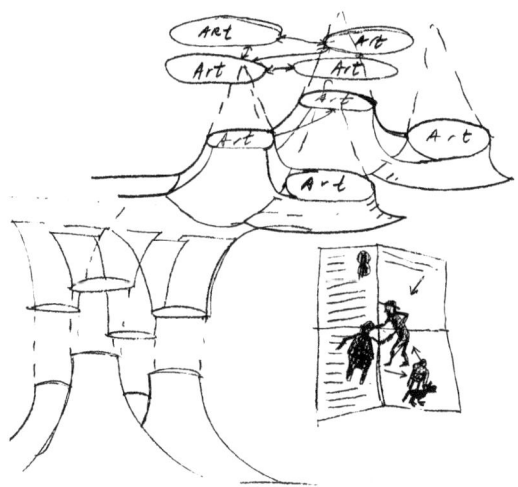

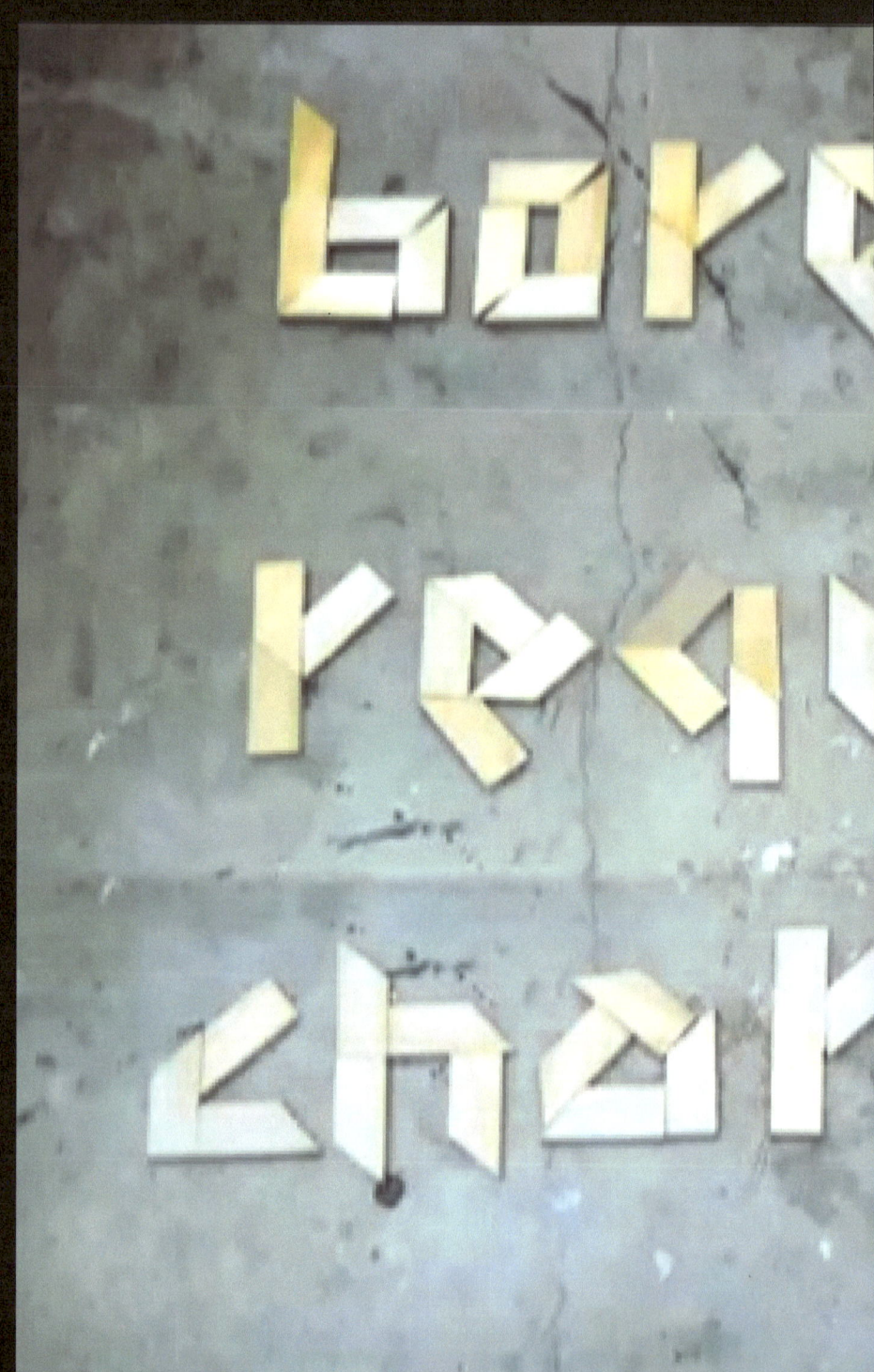

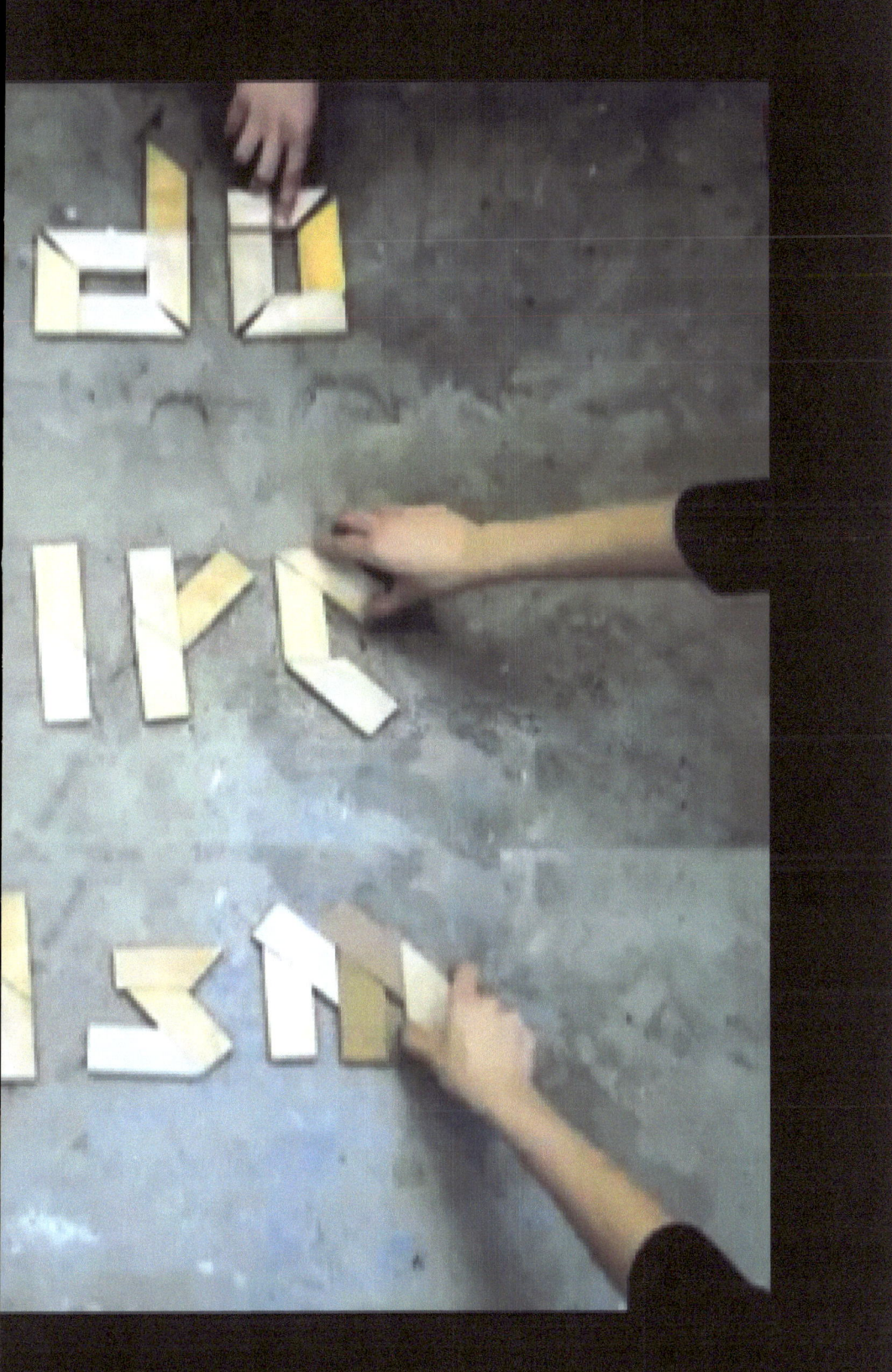

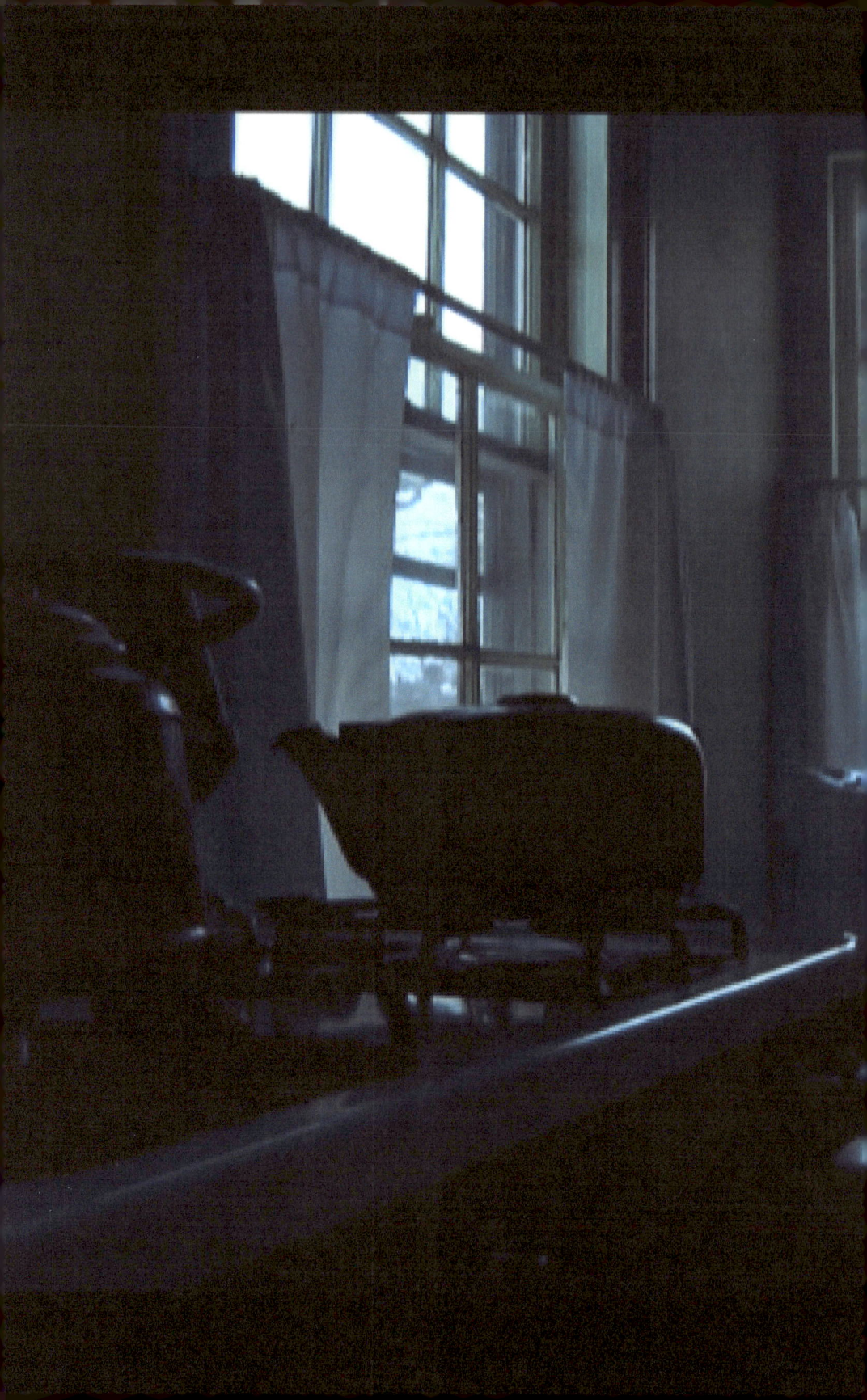

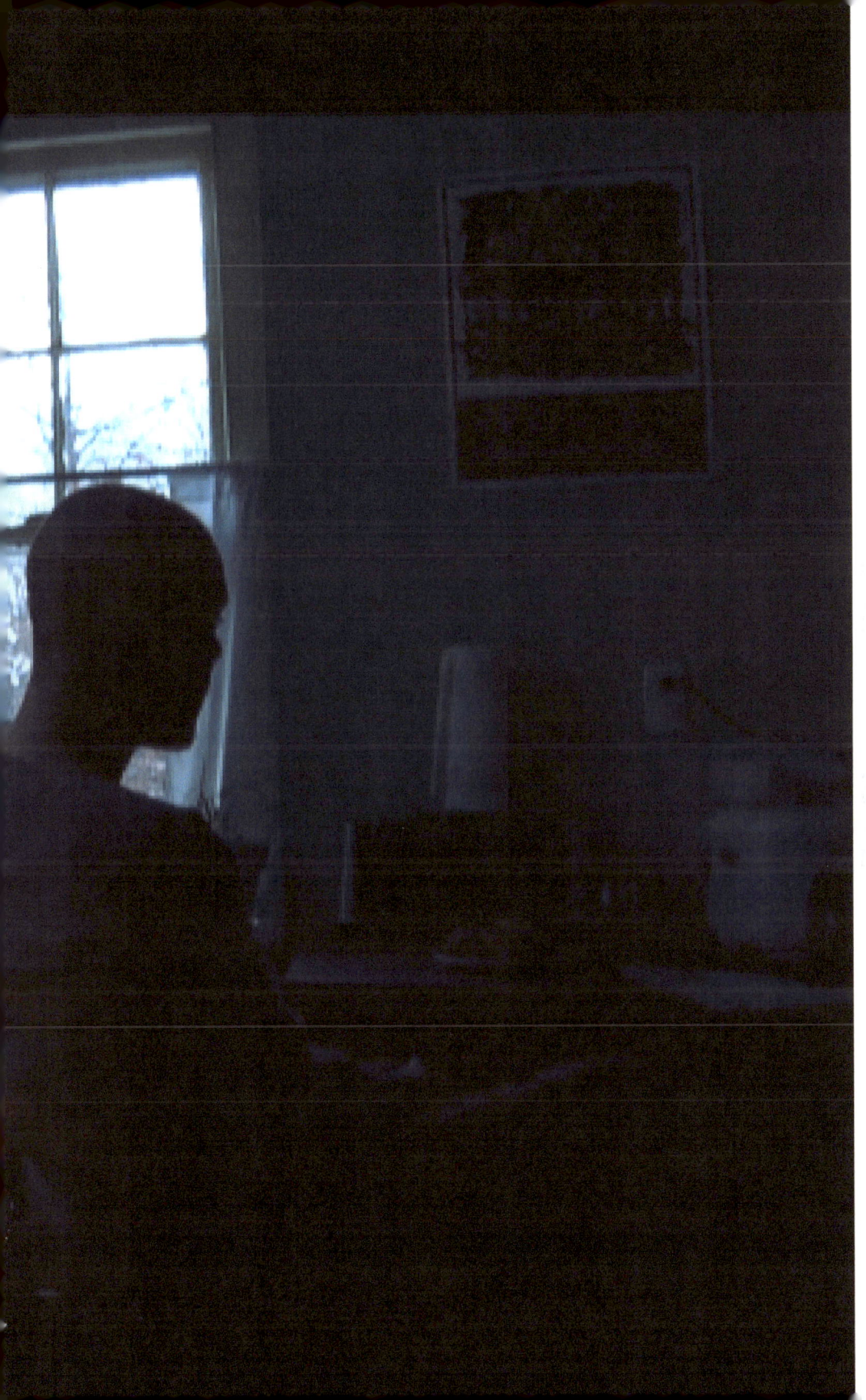

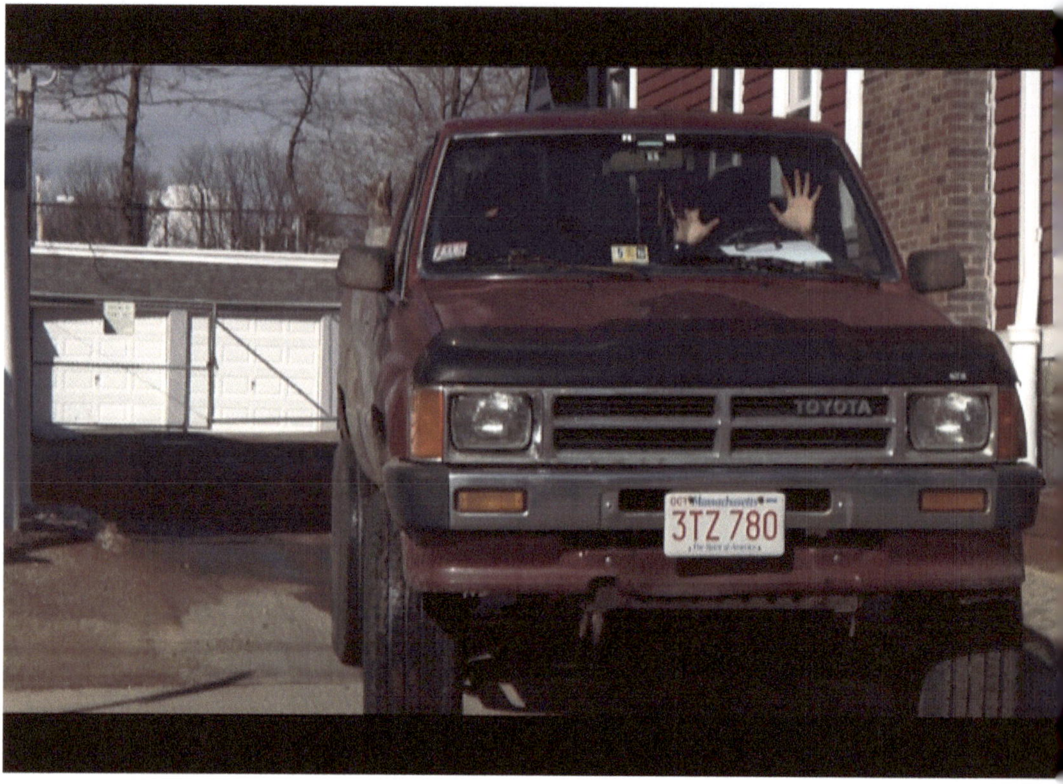
TOYOTA
3TZ 780

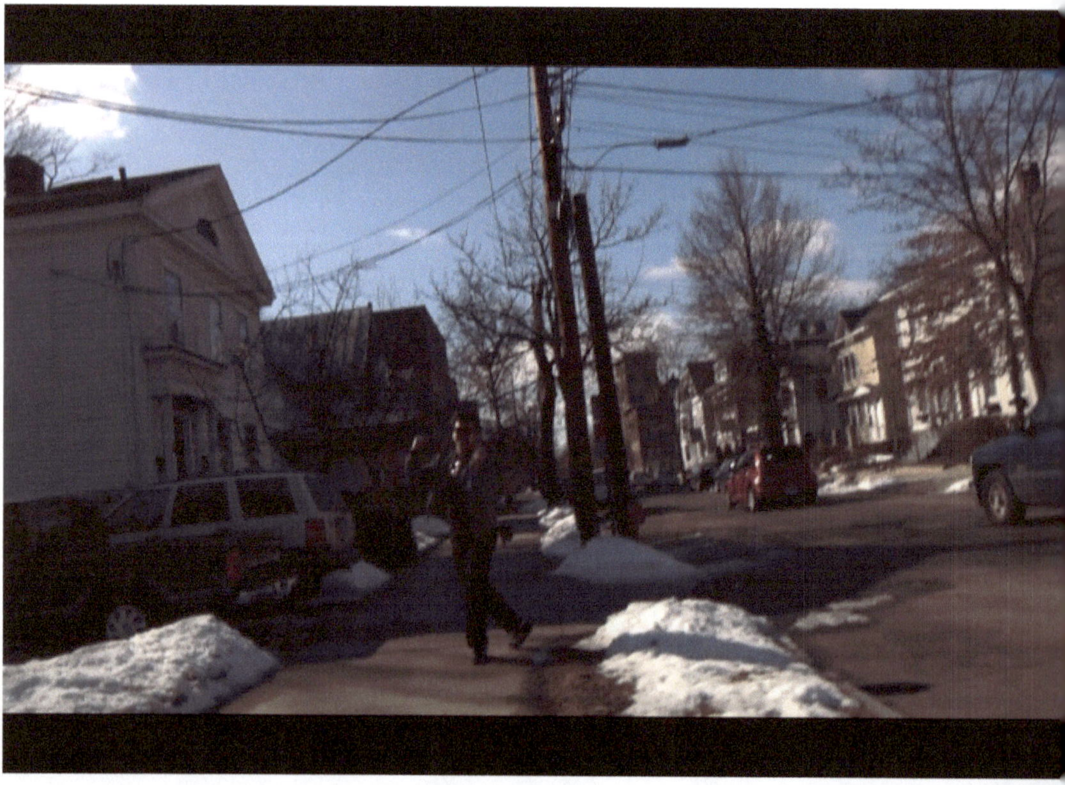

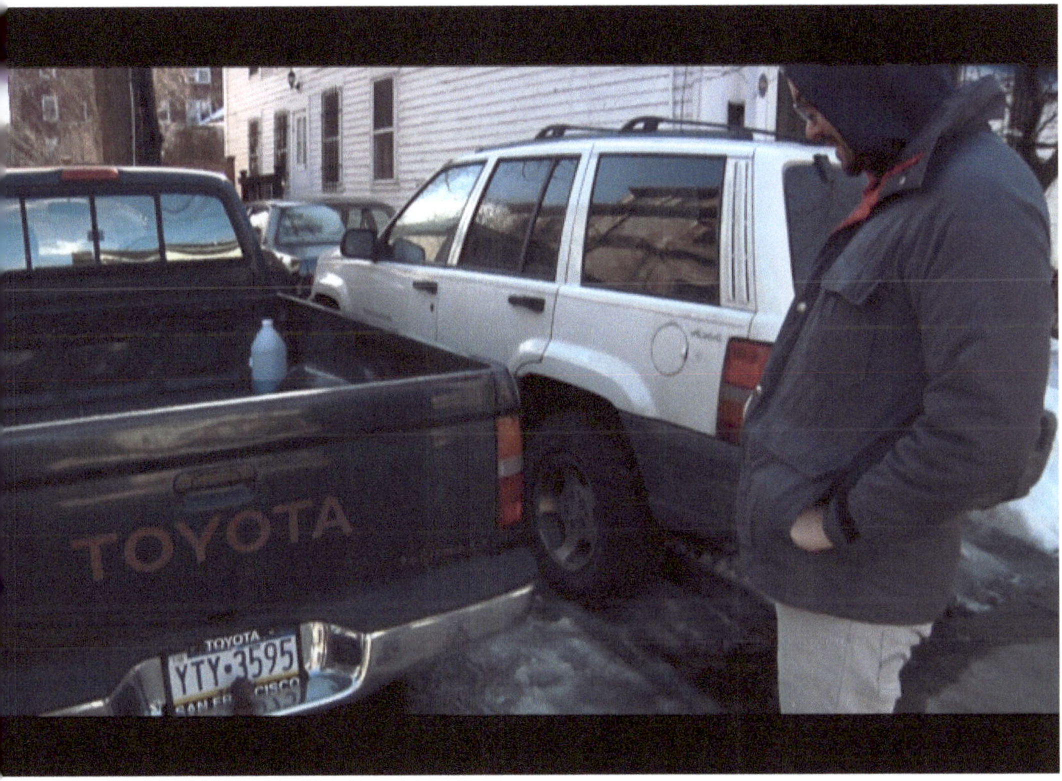
TOYOTA
TOYOTA
YTY-3595

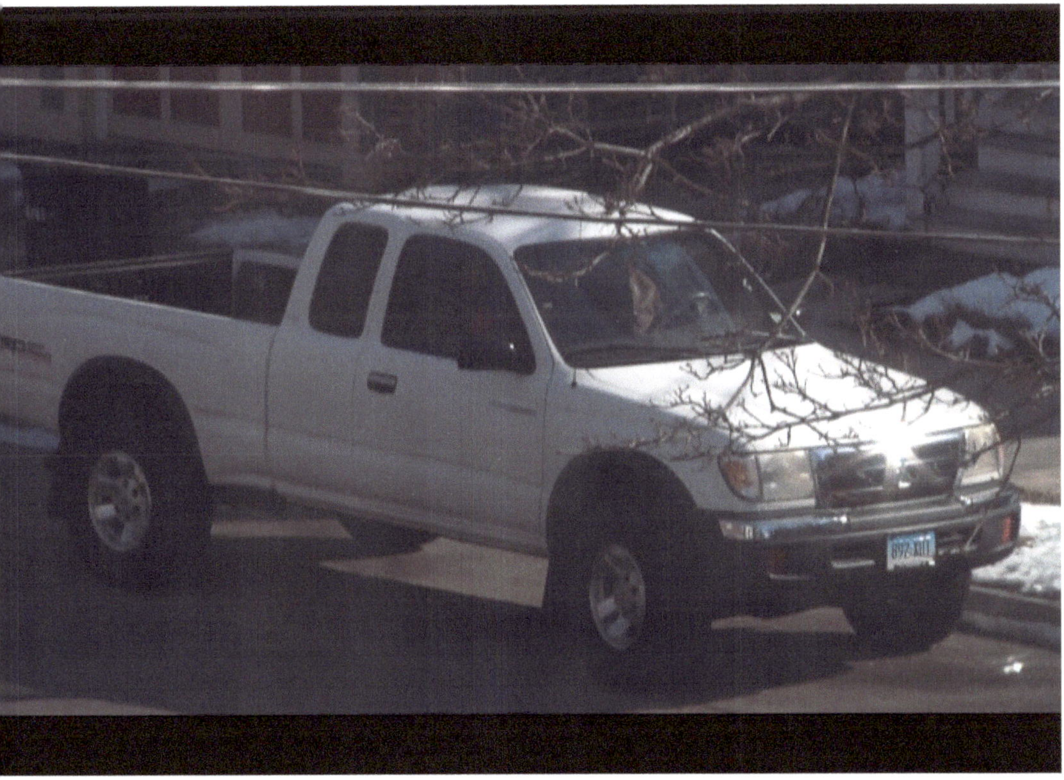

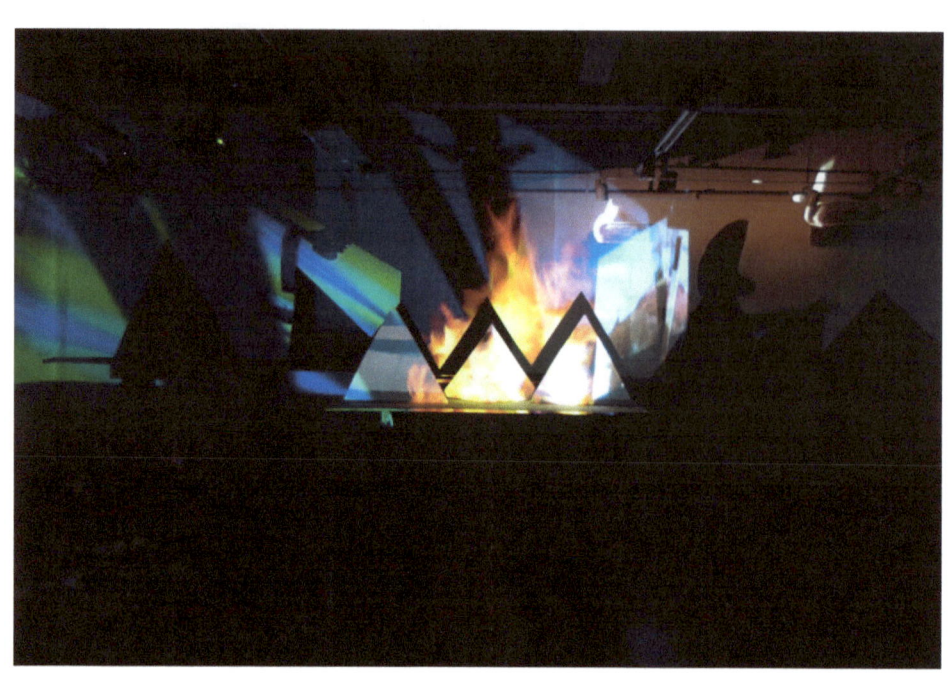

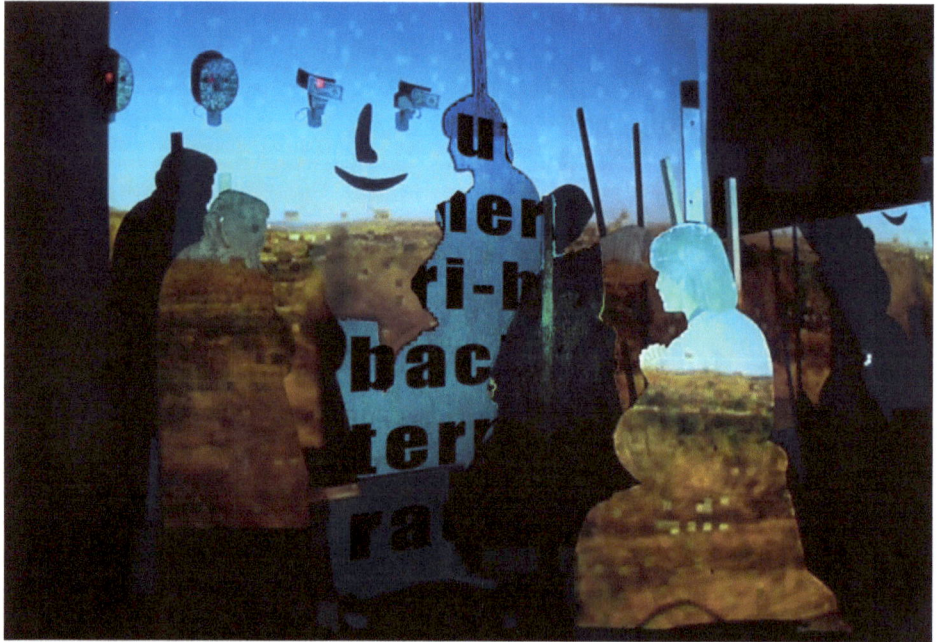

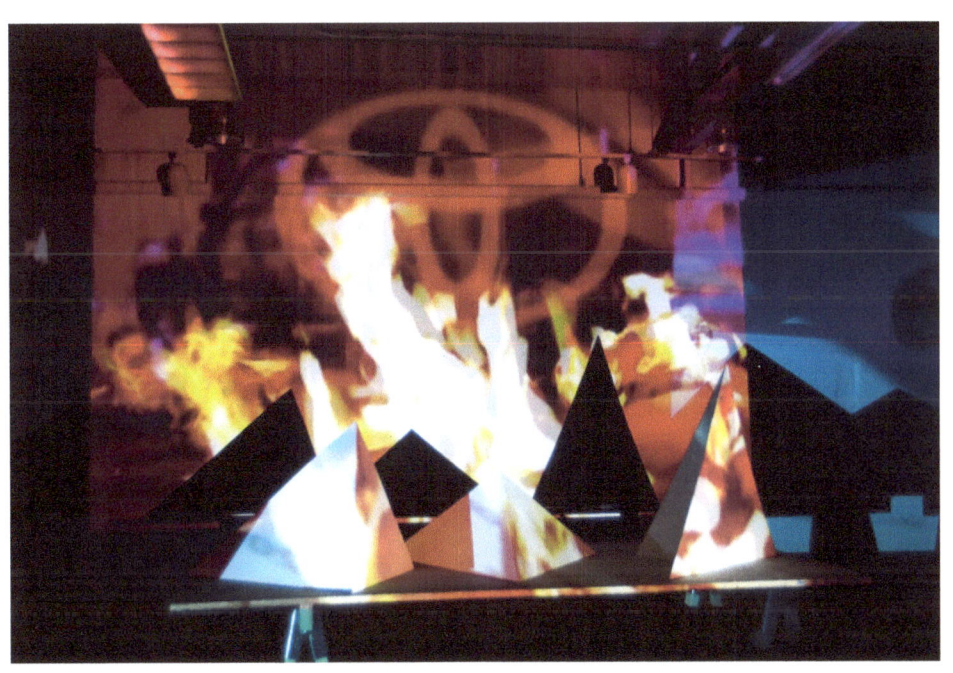

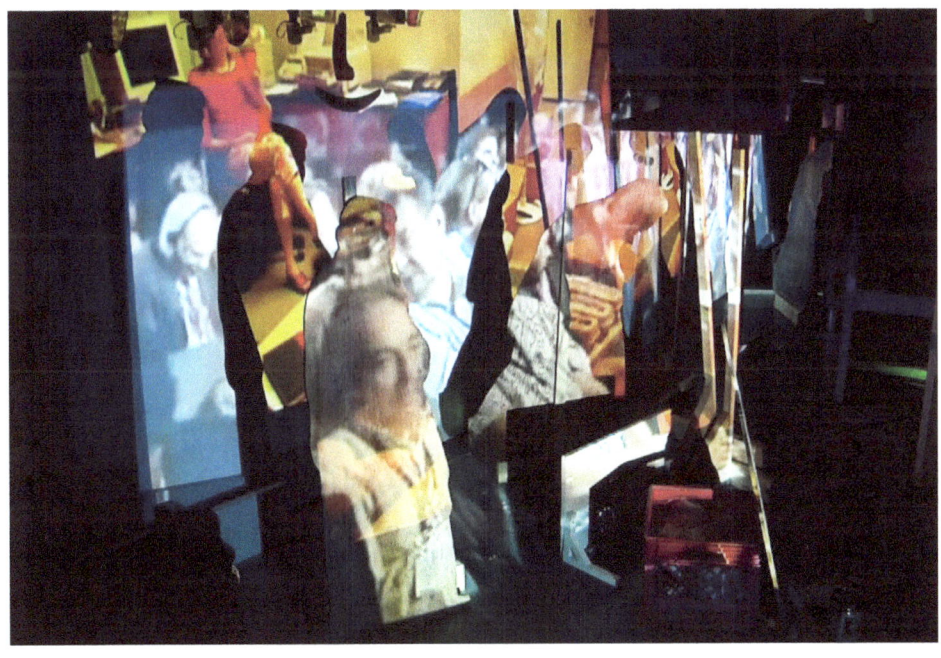

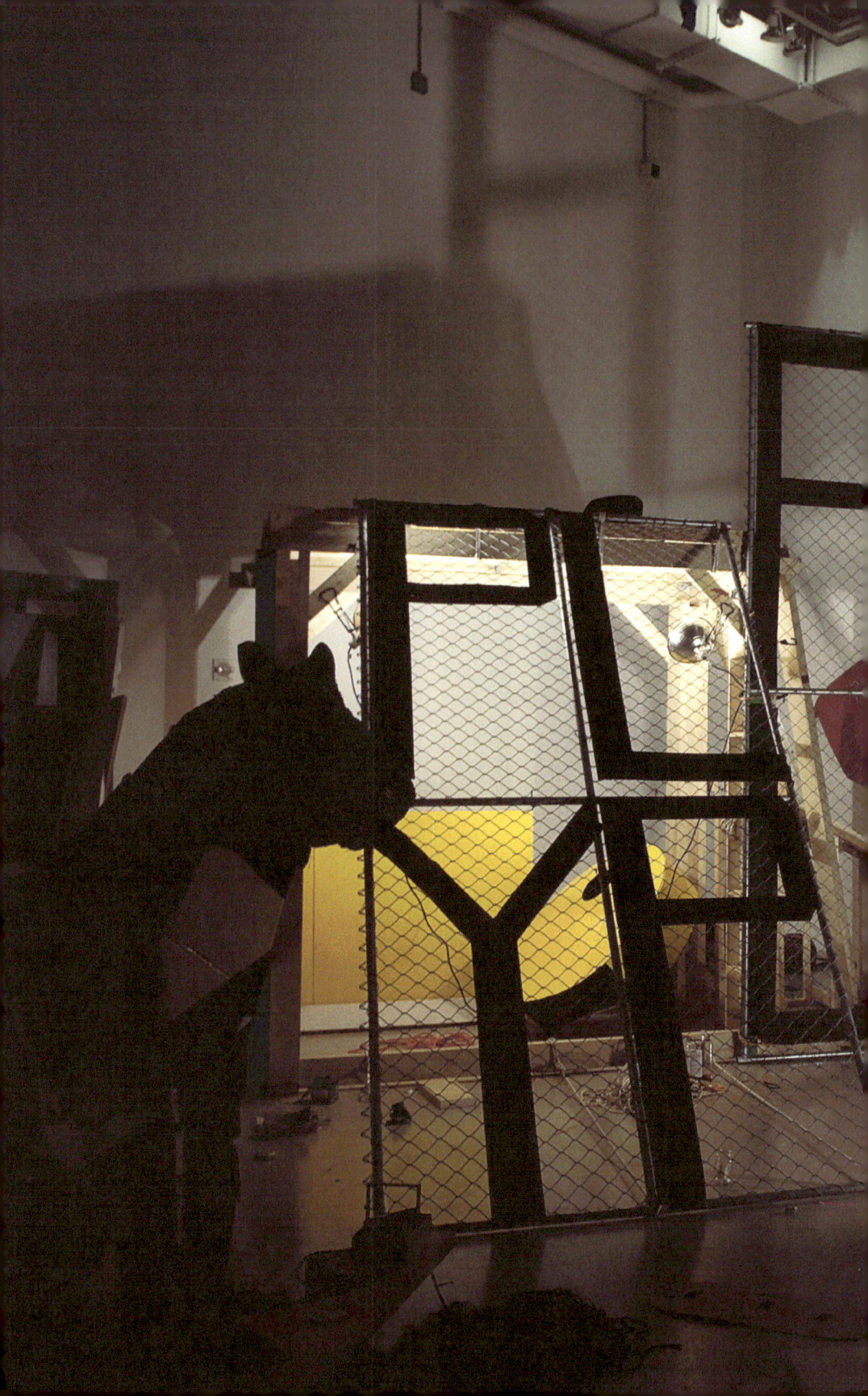

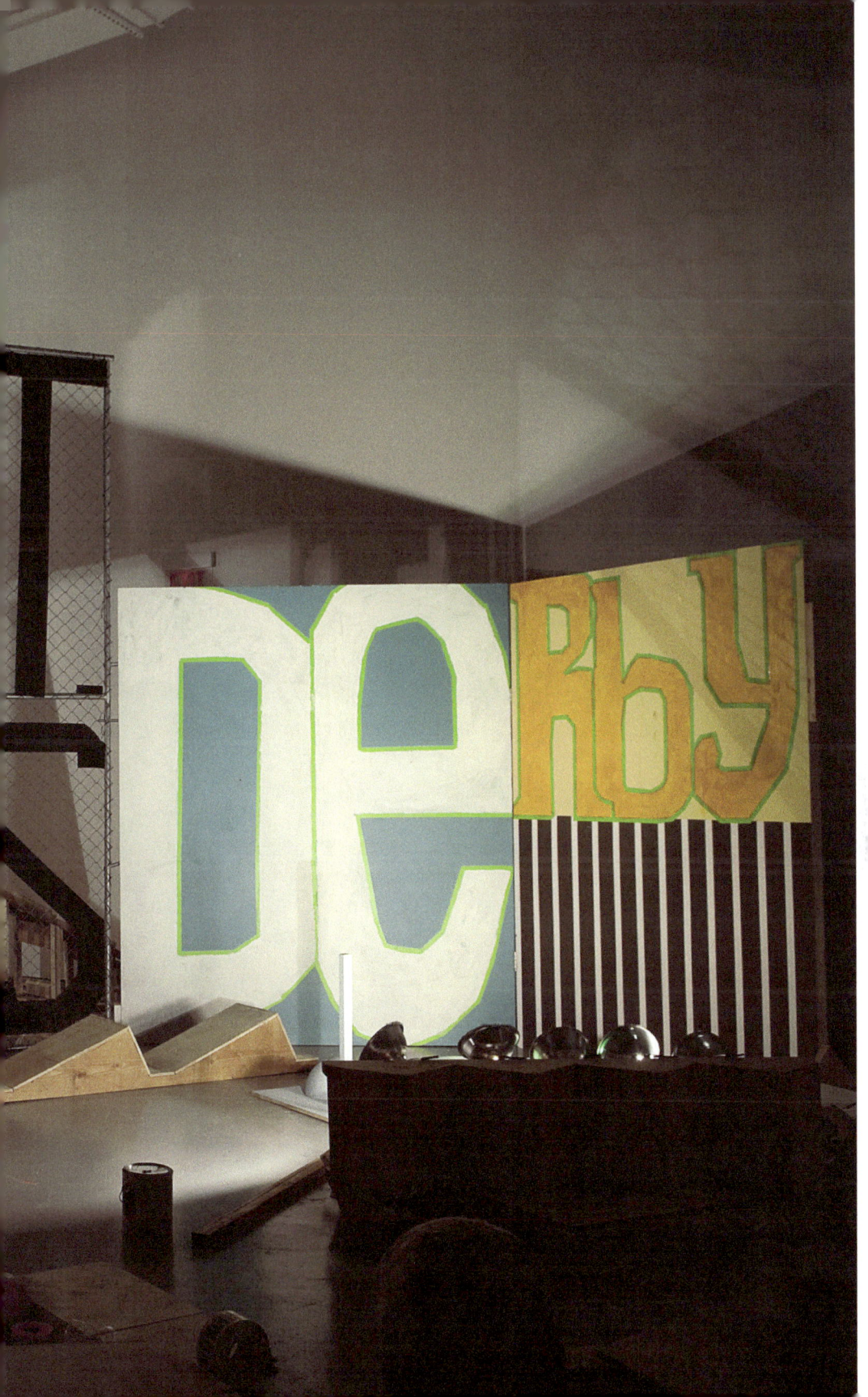

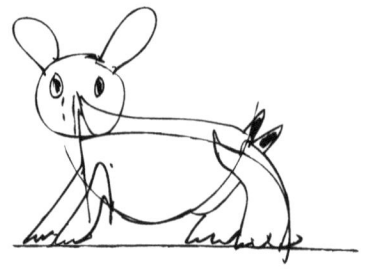

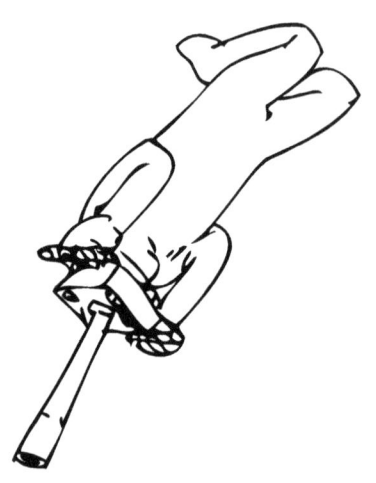

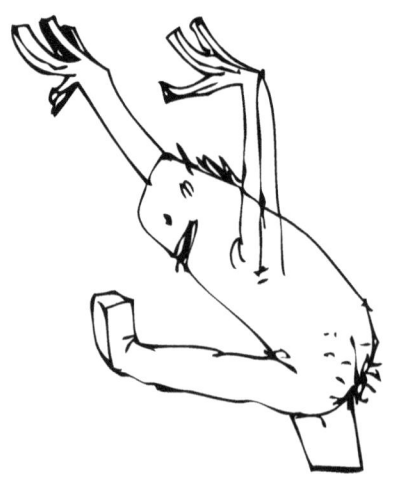

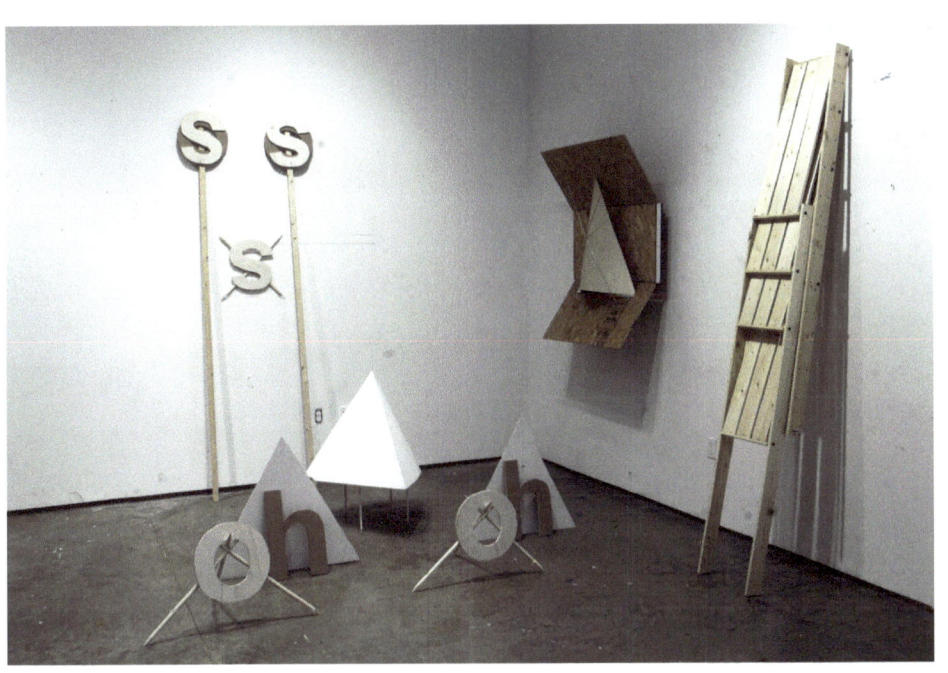

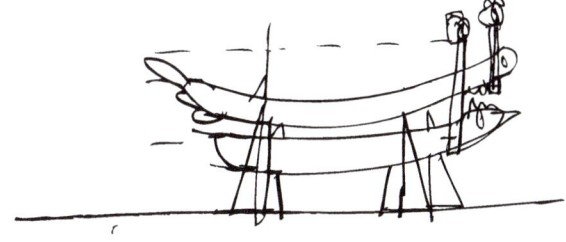

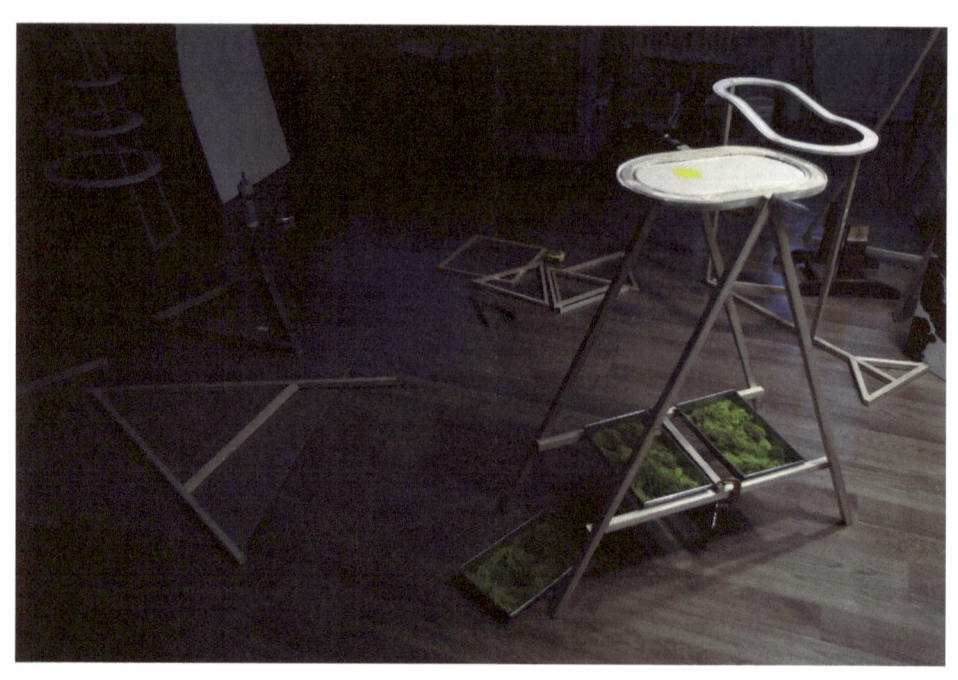

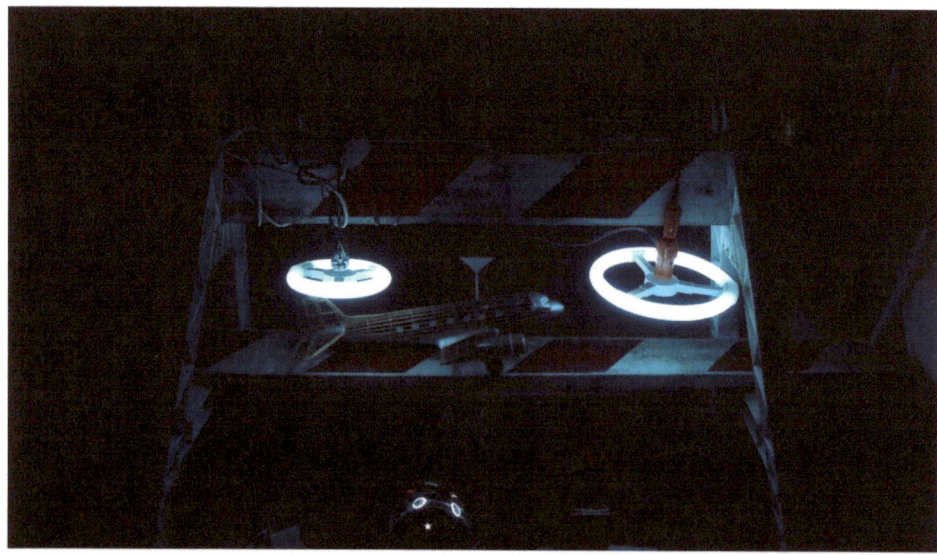

means of propagation - or tracking.
latest downloads- torrents with image files of my work.
alternative venues that also satisfies means of propagation -
or tracking.

MAC address* (safety device that can also be used against
 the consumer)
lockdown of the device* tracking
cheat games inc -games that simulate my process.
with predecided pathways that are not neccesaeily fair.

C ;

Pattern makers and system designers,
The new landscape painting of the world.
What kind of landscape are we witnessing?

The web of data created in never ending back up that mimics
quantum The web of data created in never ending back up
that mimics quantum machine is actually based on a very
fragile linkage of pipes and radio signals.Tunnels and pipes.
machine is actually based on a very fragile linkage of pipes
and radio signals.

Tunnels and pipes.Data landscapes.
I can't help but notice some similarities in information
design and landscape paintings. The future of internet,
like cloud computing is pictured in my head as German
sublime landscape painting. Where lone individual is facing,
contemplating or deserted in vast nature. Although the data
can be stored in the clouds up in the sky, it relies on a physical
product, by cutting down the connection between data's flow
the information can disappear.
I will take on the idea and explore ways of presenting such
connections as a traditional medium, such as drawings, and
ideally I'd like to produce a router that I would place a piece
of firmware that enables to shut down specific product that
has connection to the net.

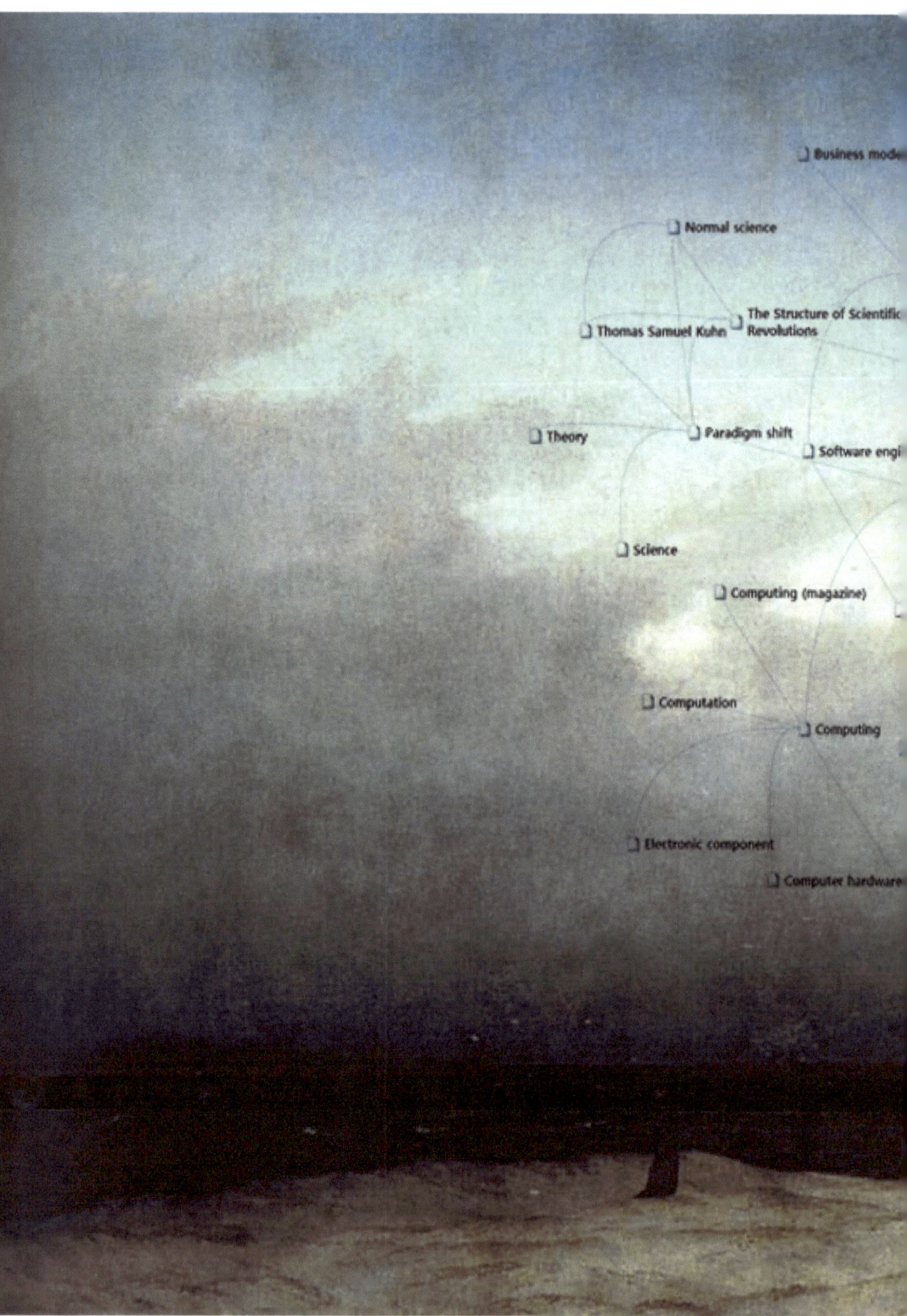

Business mode

Normal science

Thomas Samuel Kuhn   The Structure of Scientific
Revolutions

Theory   Paradigm shift

Software engi

Science

Computing (magazine)

Computation

Computing

Electronic component

Computer hardware

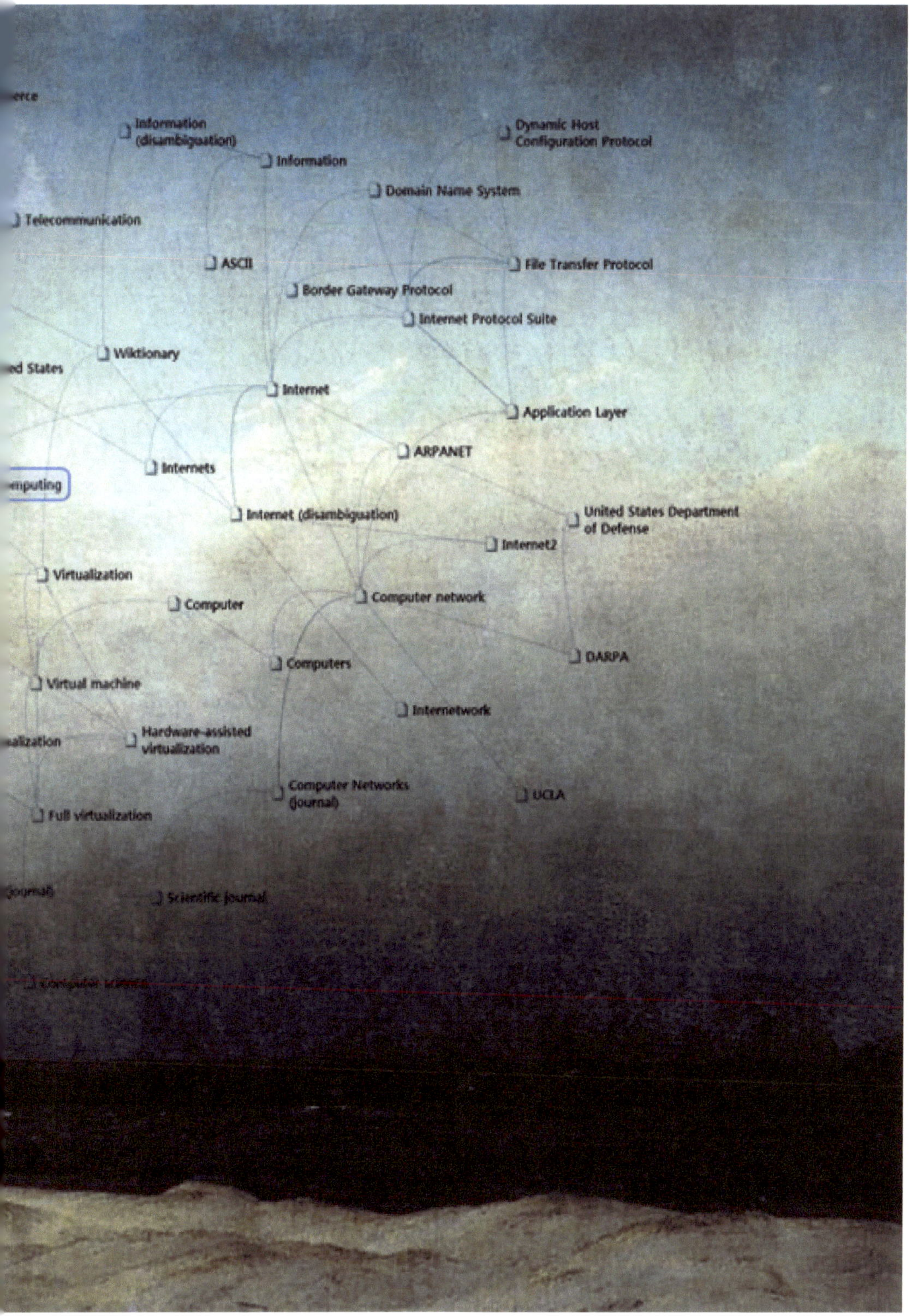

erce

Information
(disambiguation)

Information

Dynamic Host
Configuration Protocol

Telecommunication

Domain Name System

ASCII

File Transfer Protocol

Border Gateway Protocol

Internet Protocol Suite

Wiktionary

ed States

Internet

Application Layer

ARPANET

Internets

mputing

Internet (disambiguation)

United States Department
of Defense

Internet2

Virtualization

Computer

Computer network

Virtual machine

Computers

DARPA

Hardware-assisted
virtualization

Internetwork

alization

Full virtualization

Computer Networks
(journal)

UCLA

(journal)

Scientific journal

Computer science

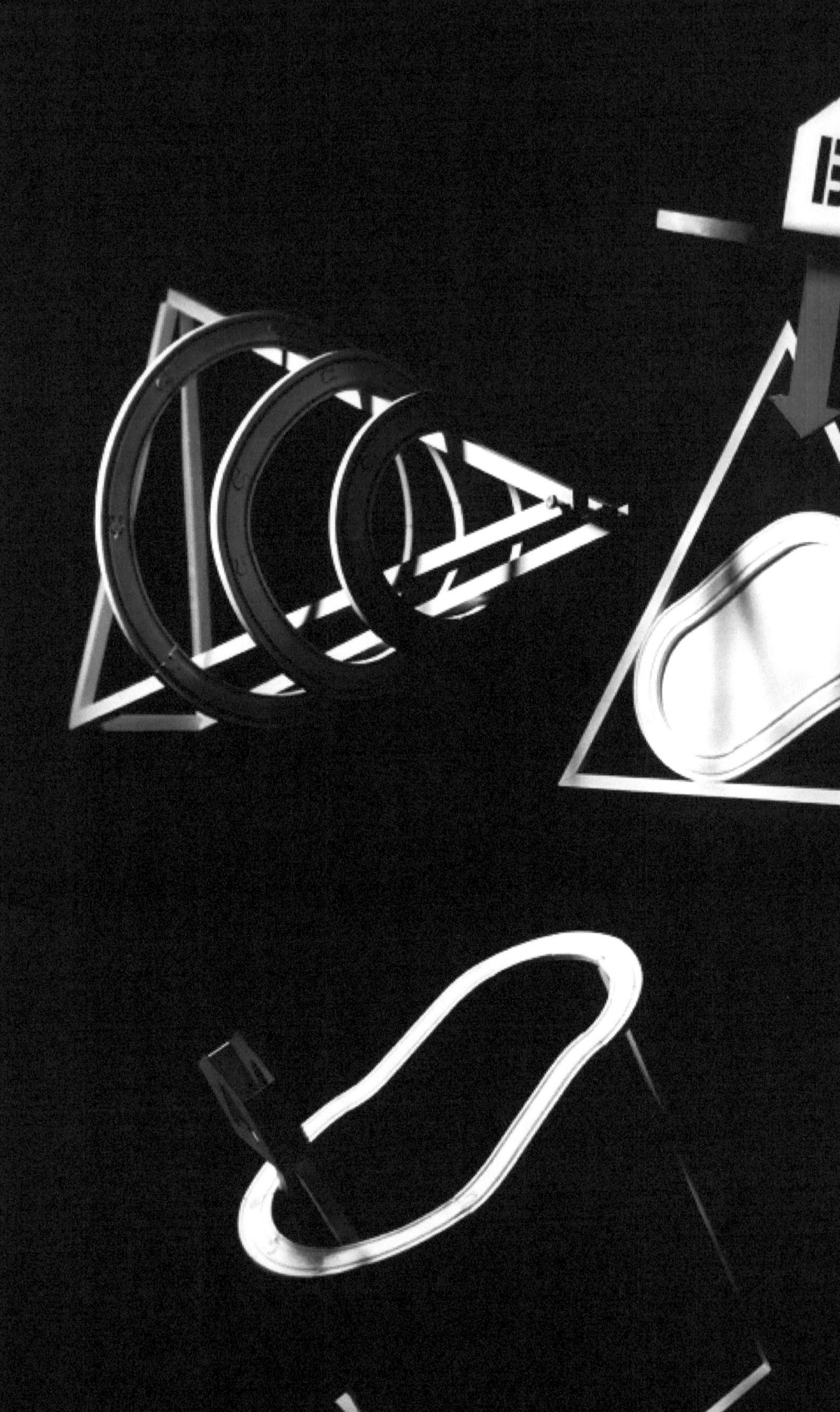

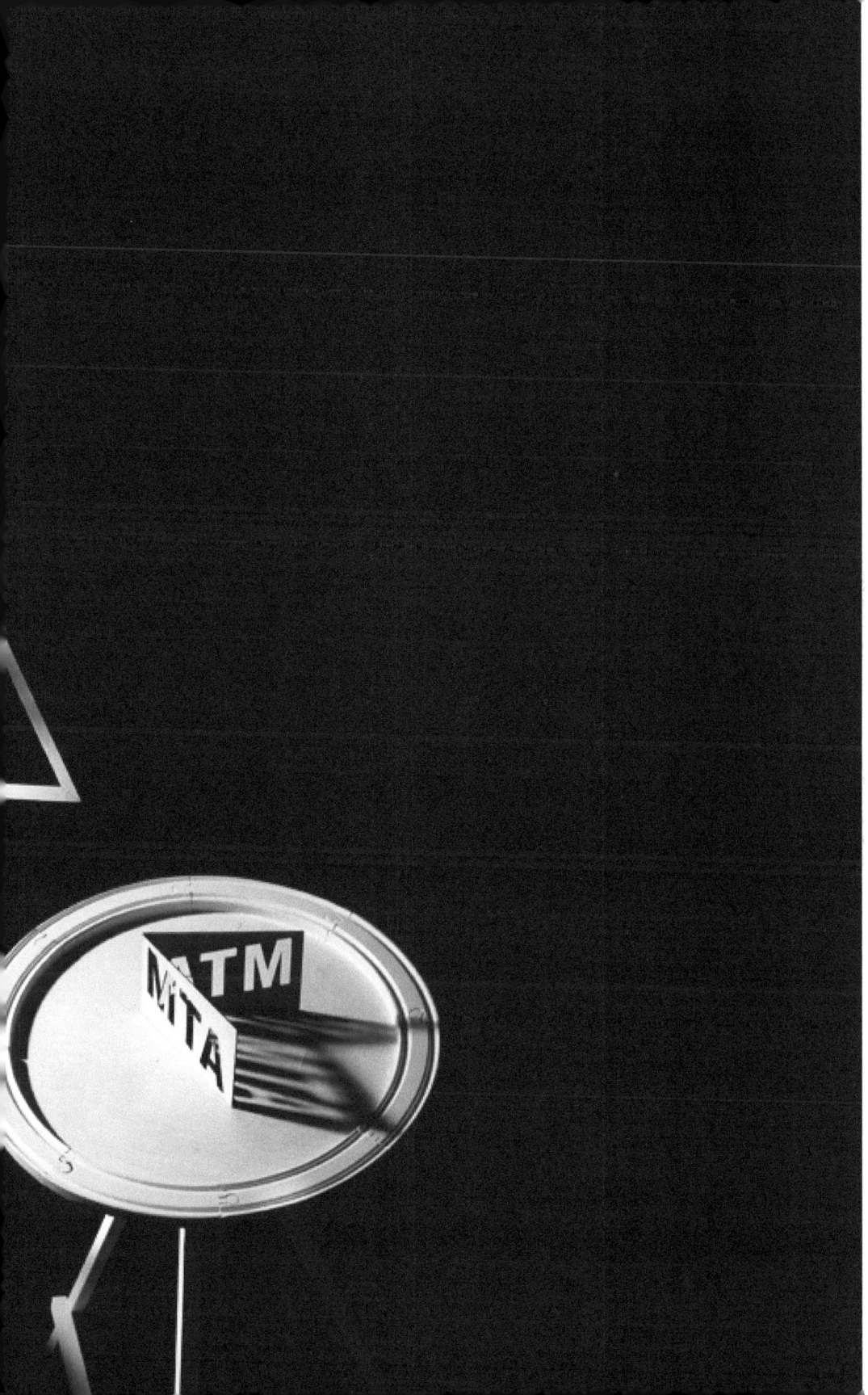

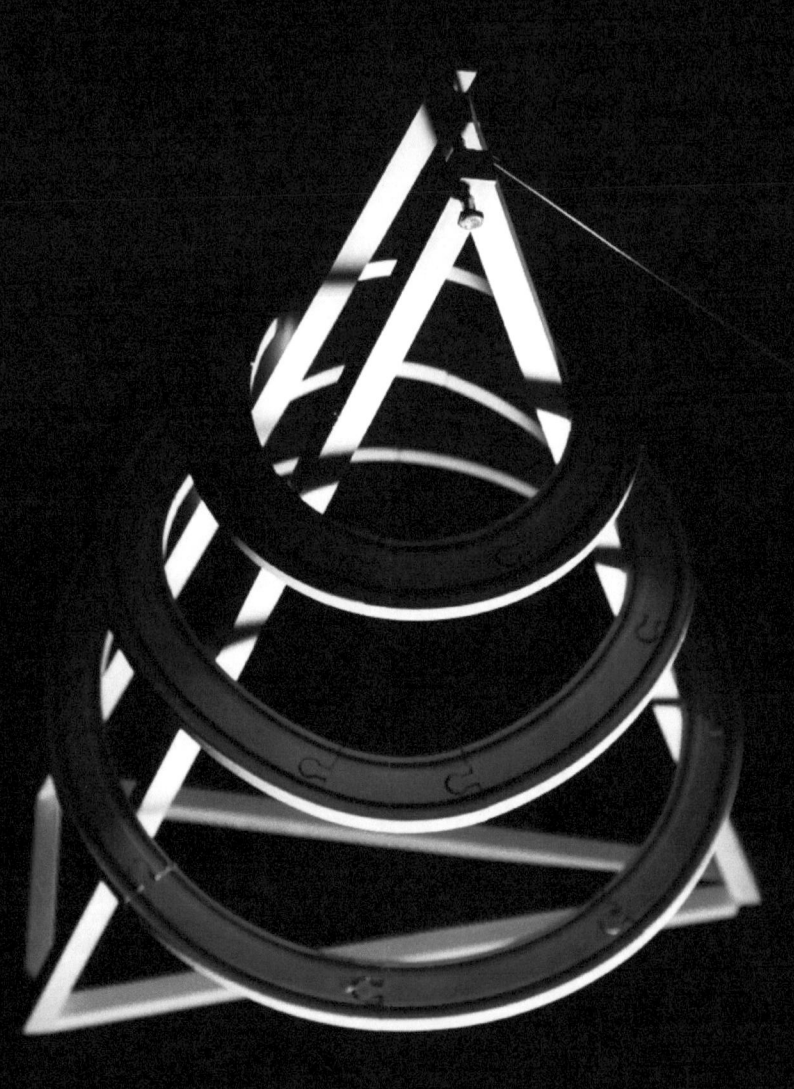

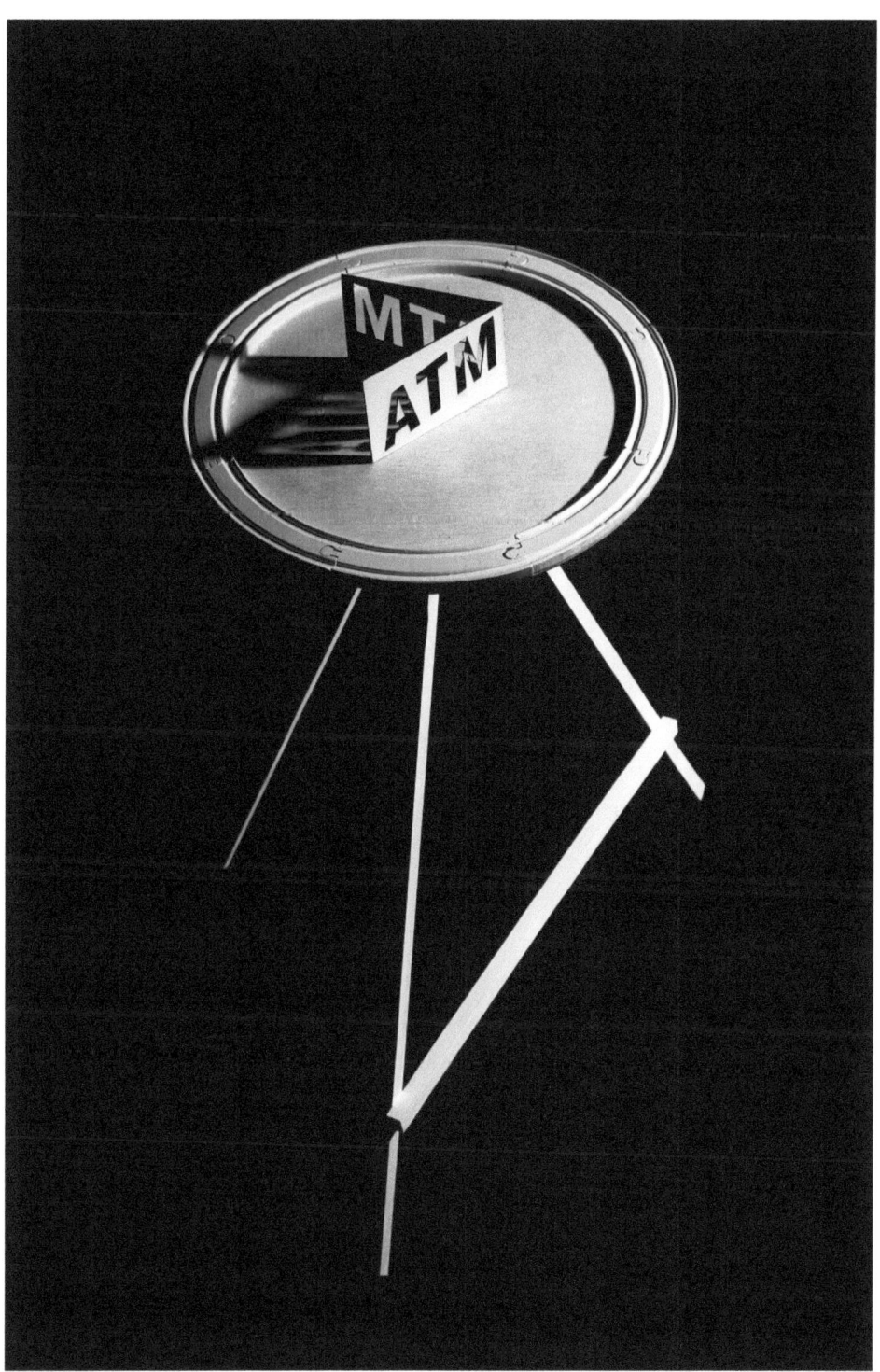

Photo: Ahrong Han

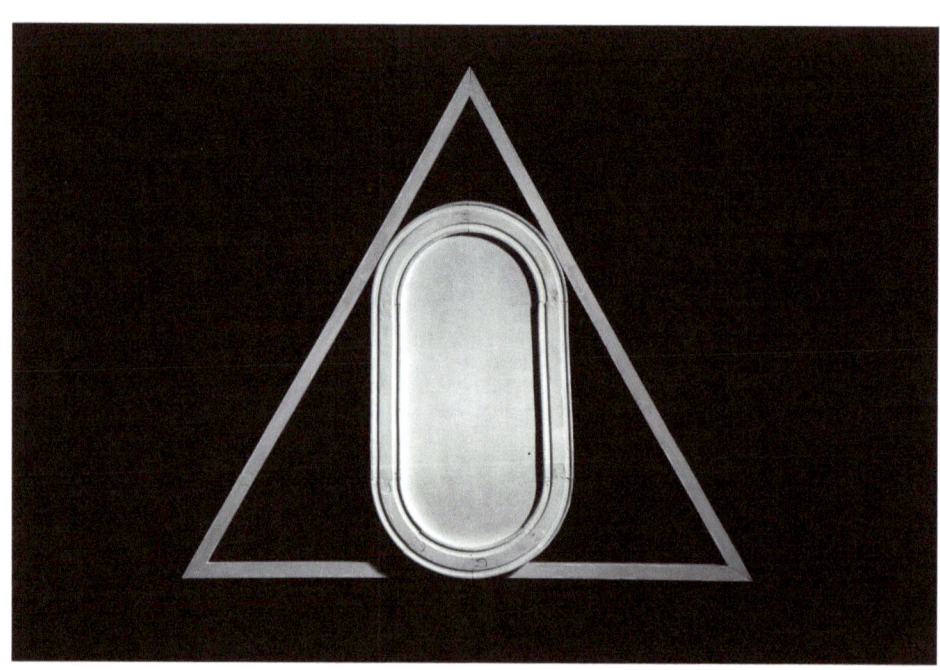

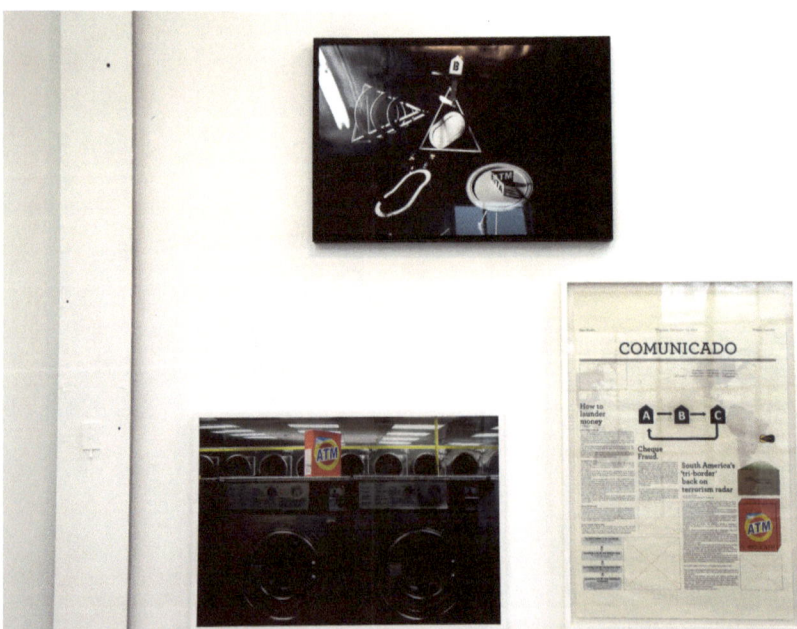

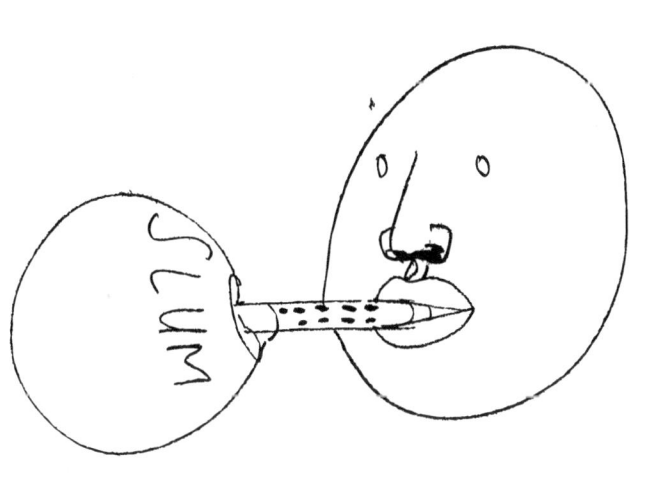

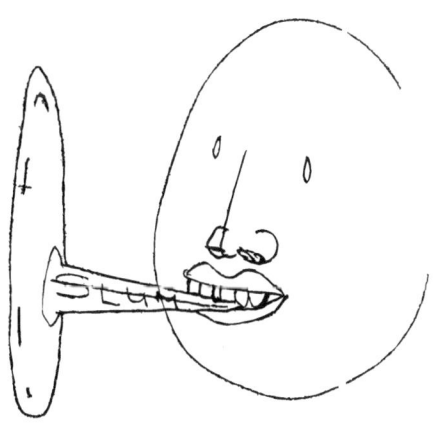

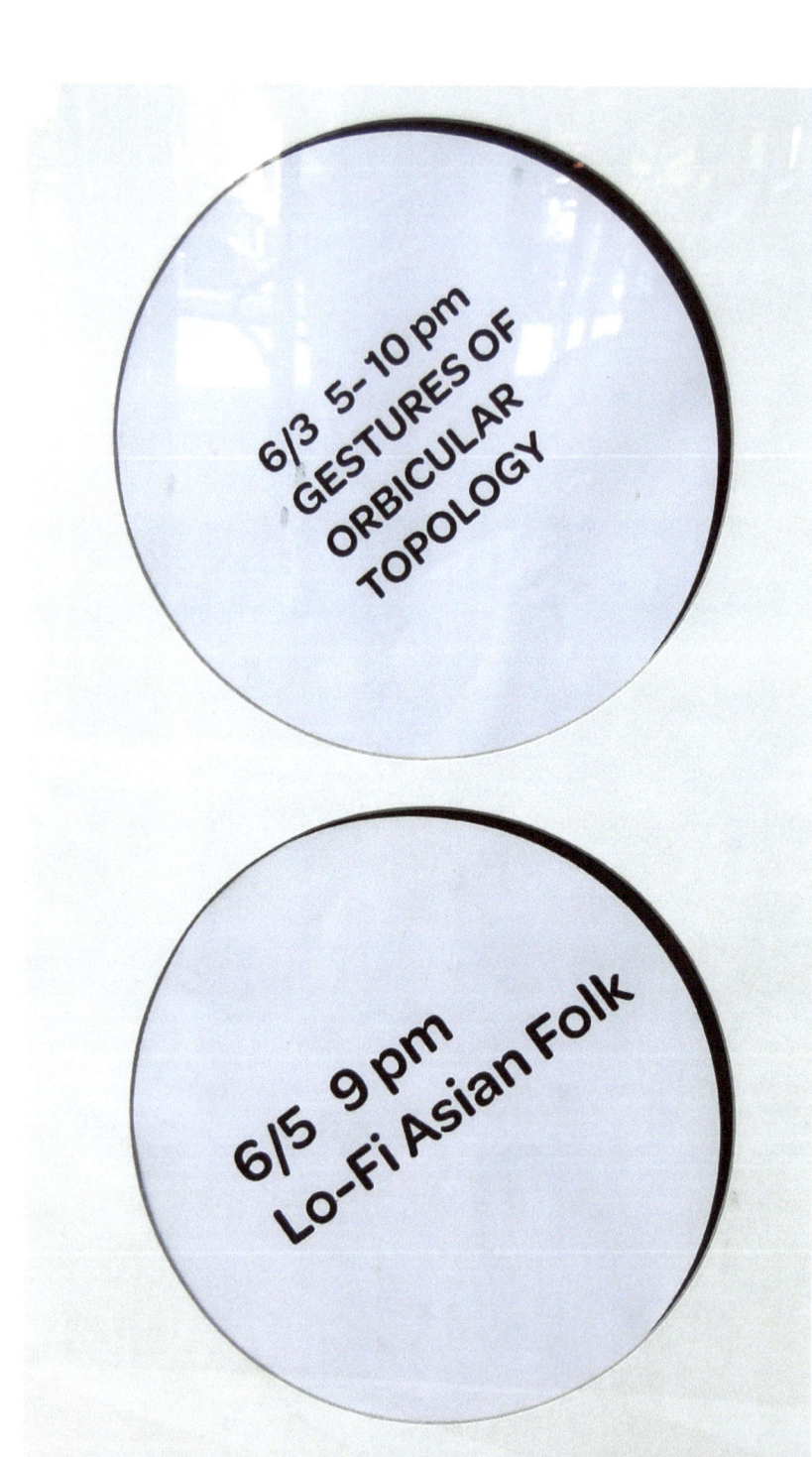

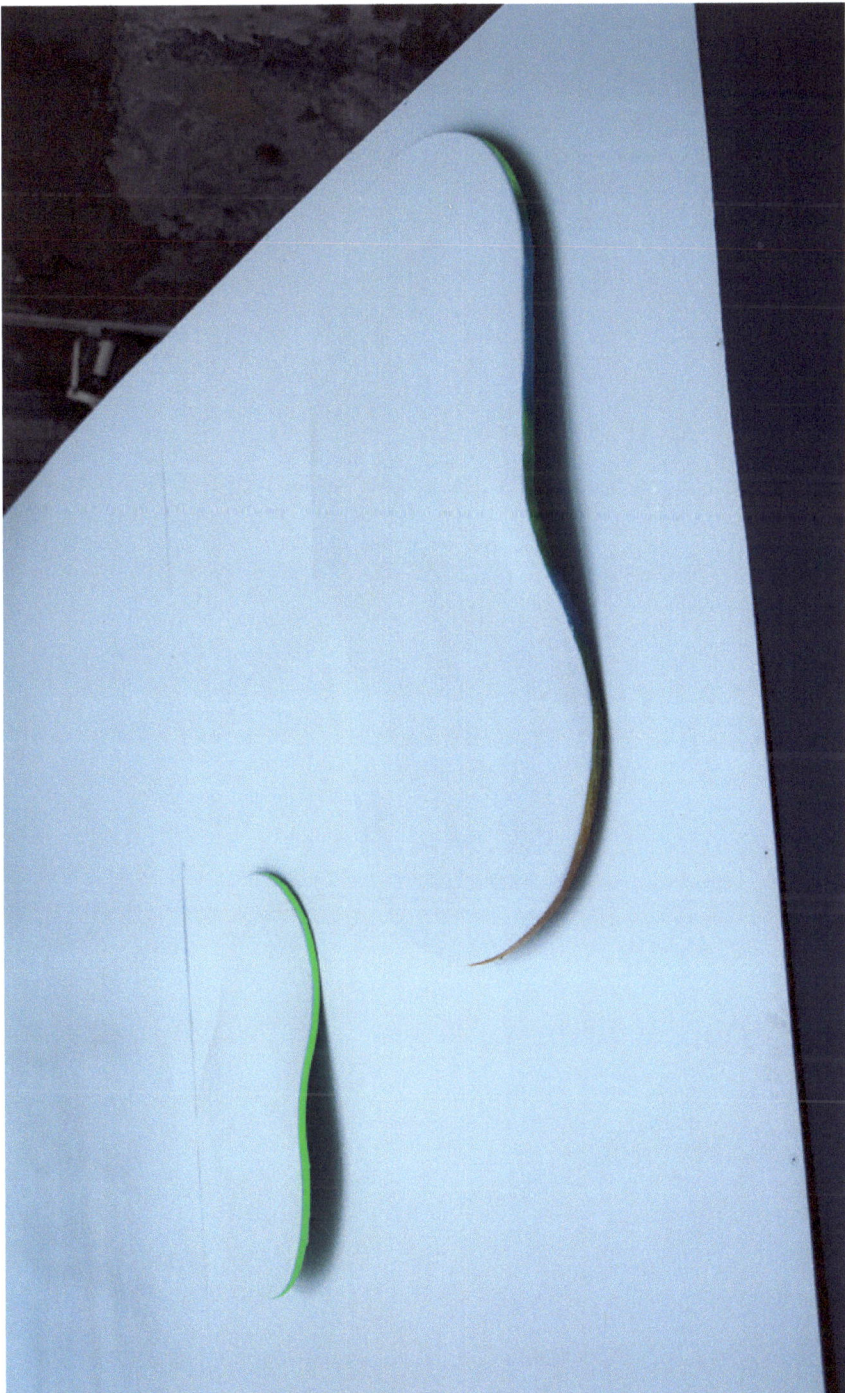

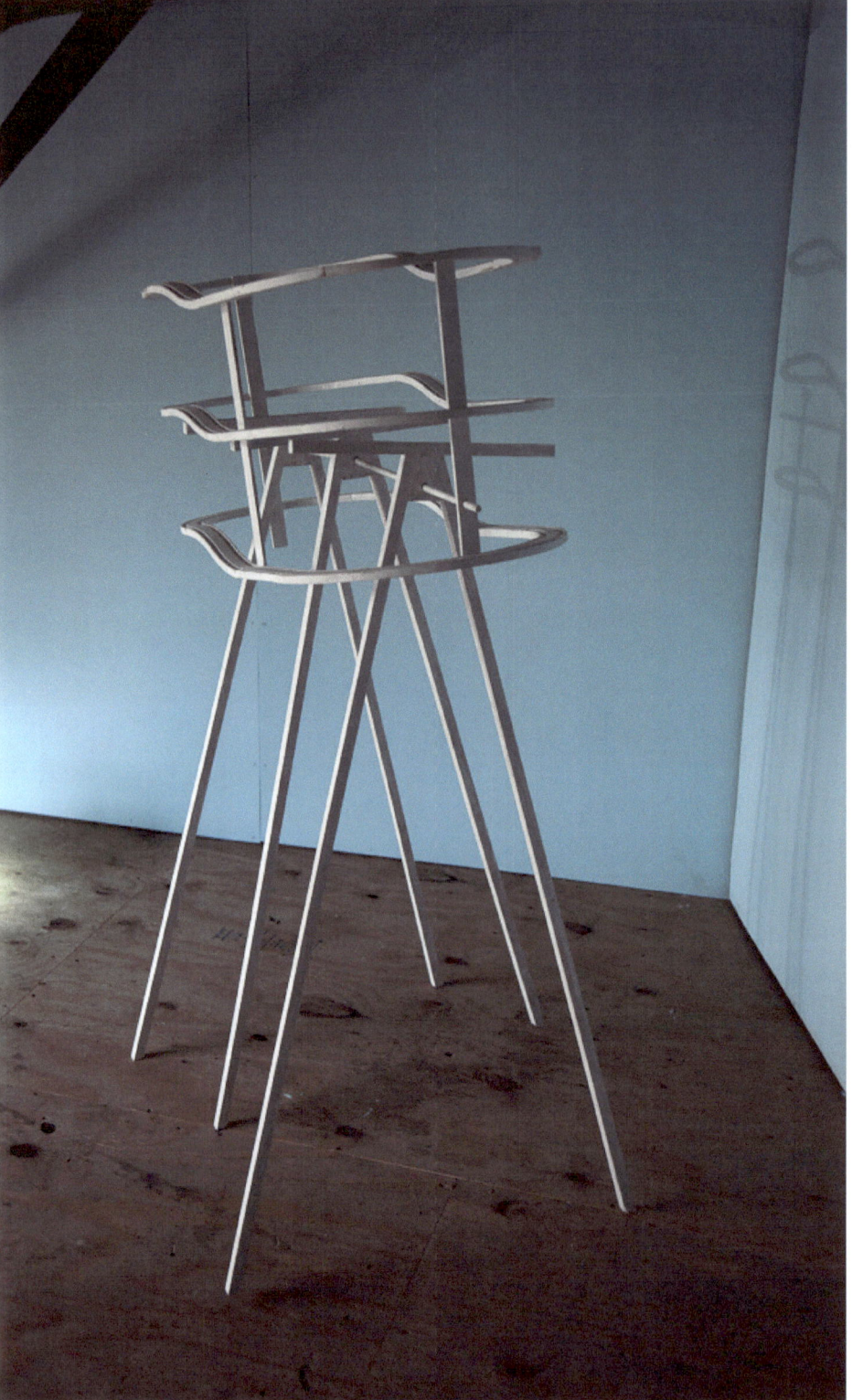

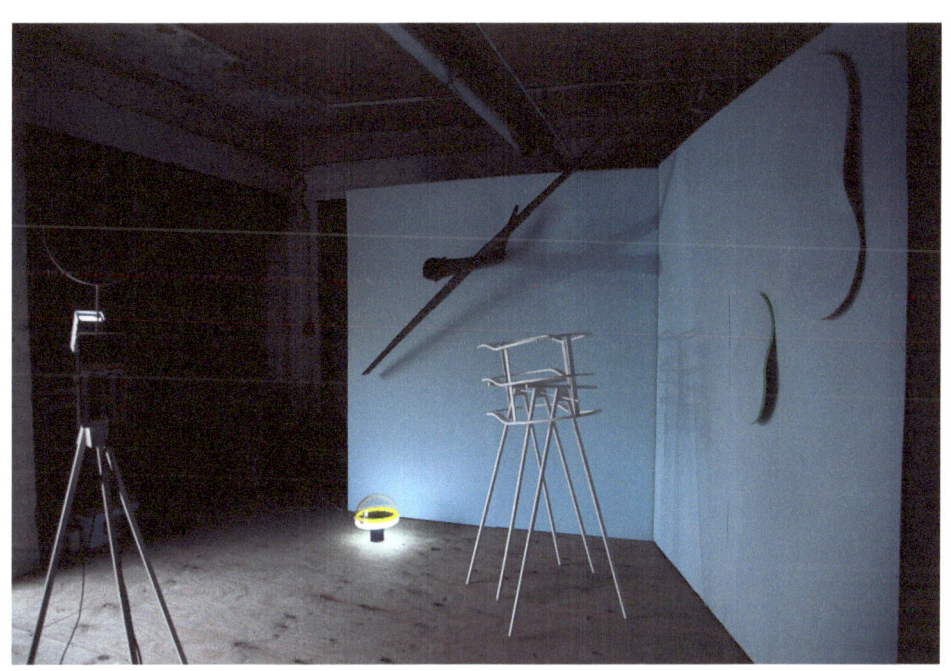

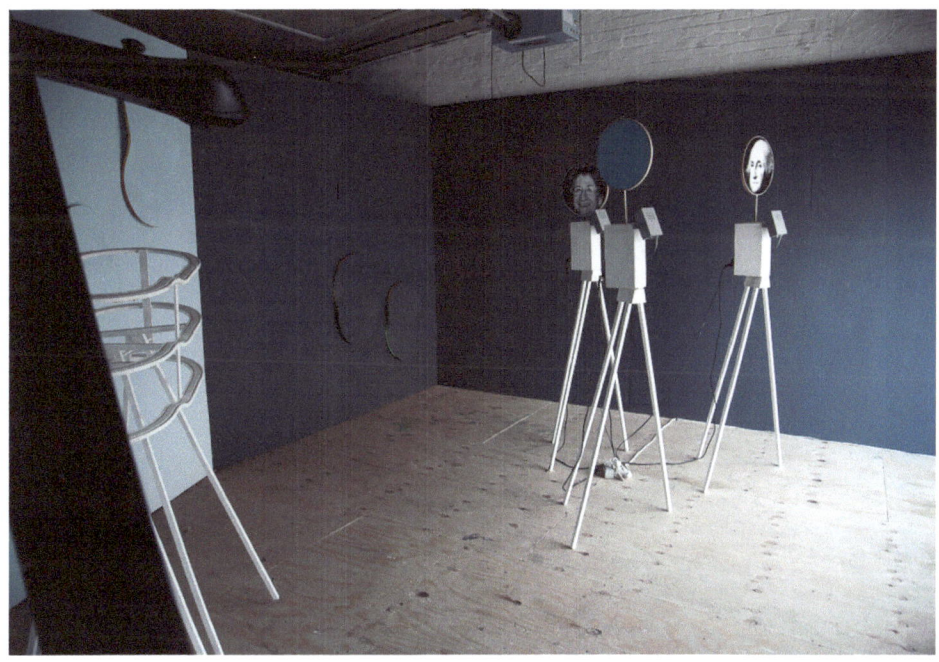

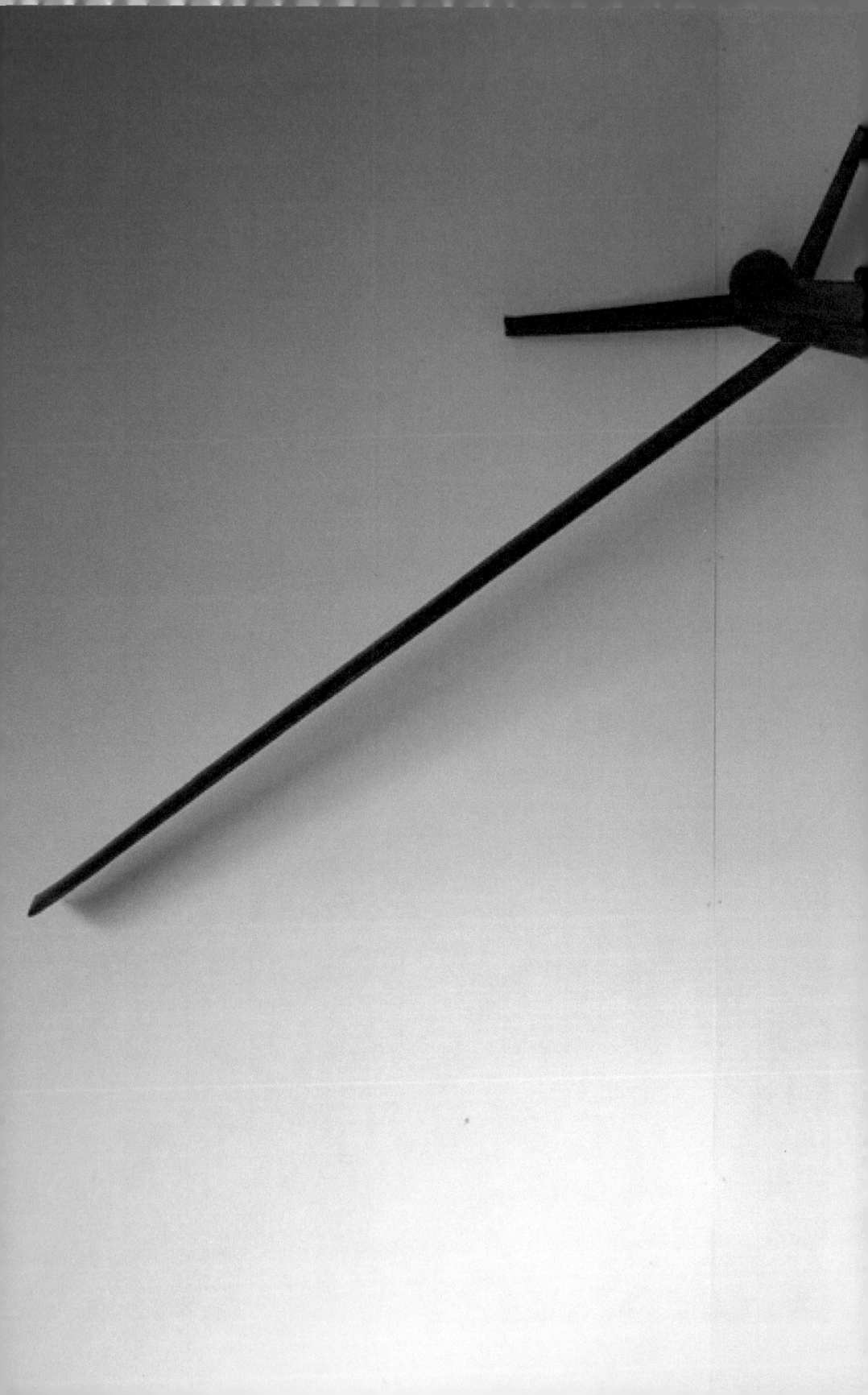

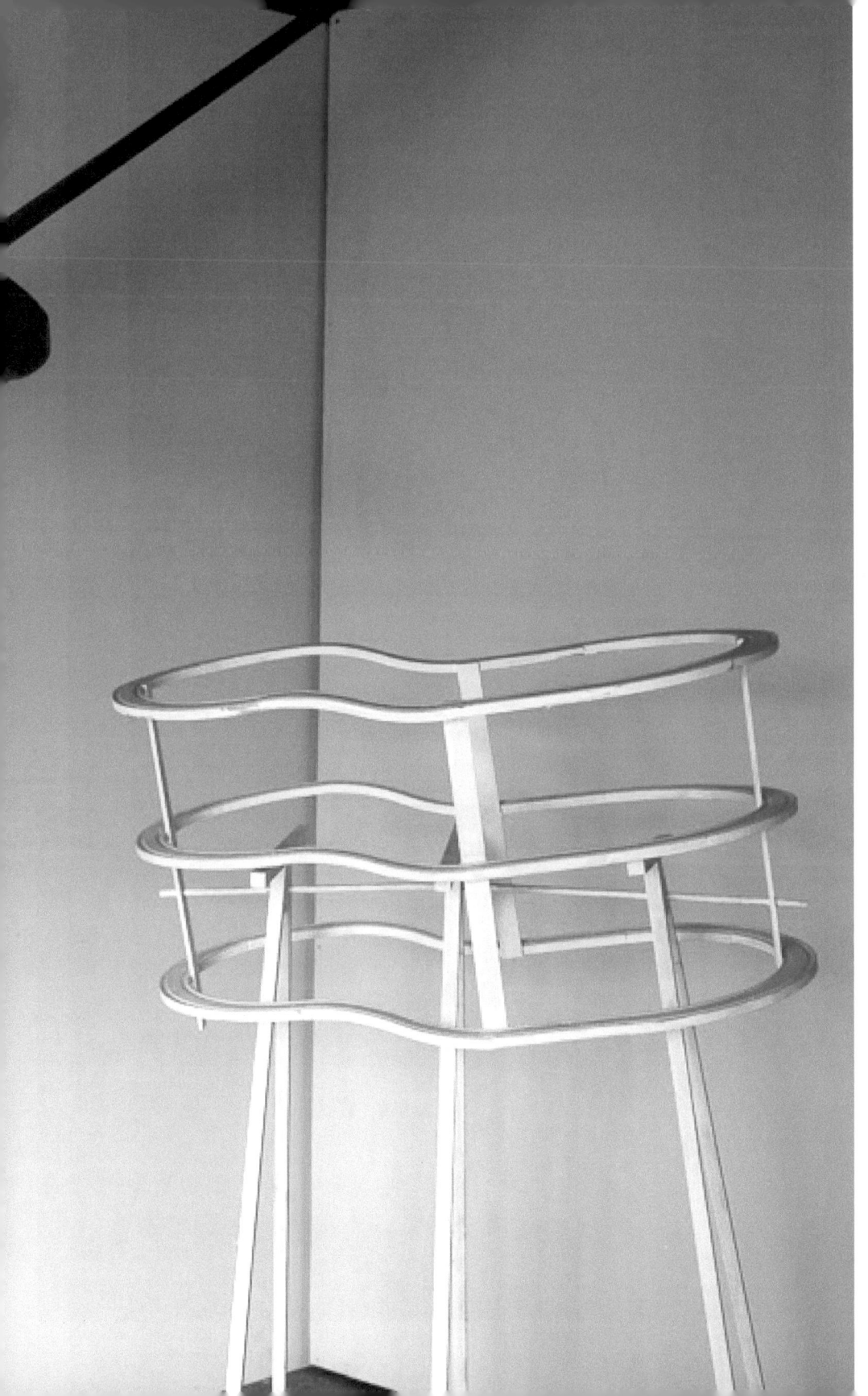

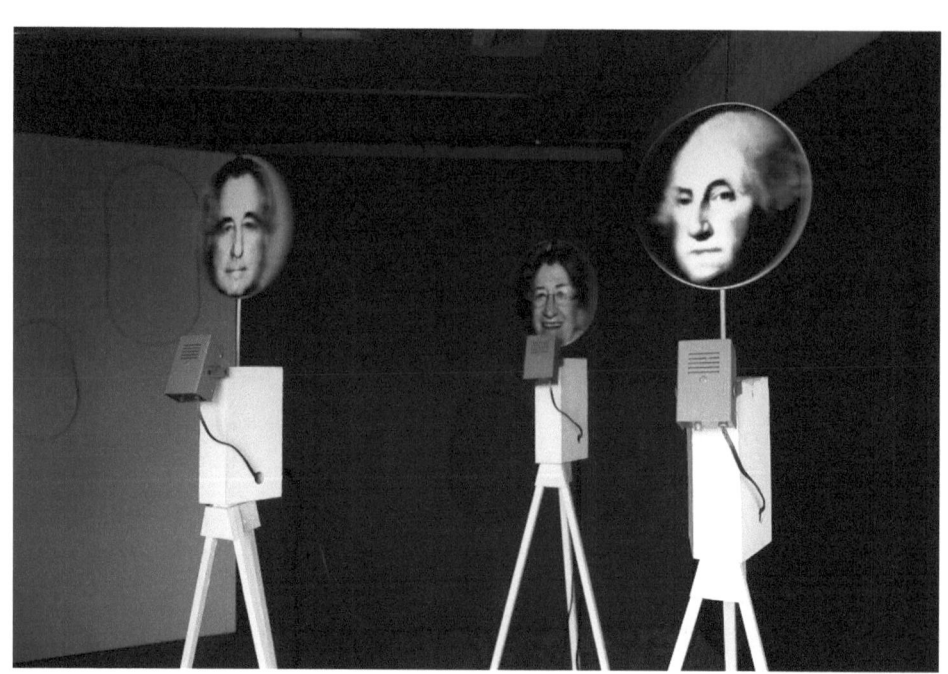

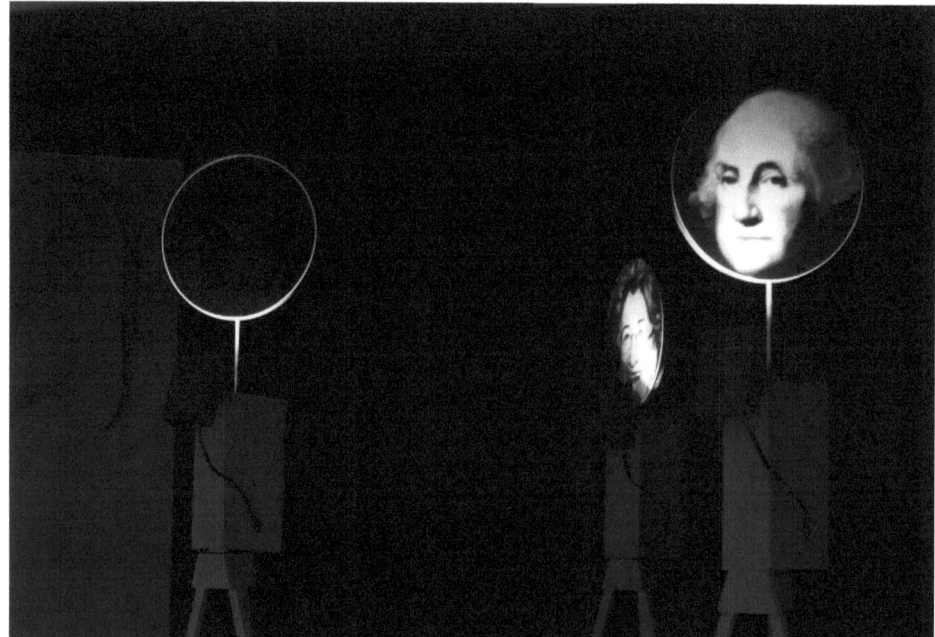

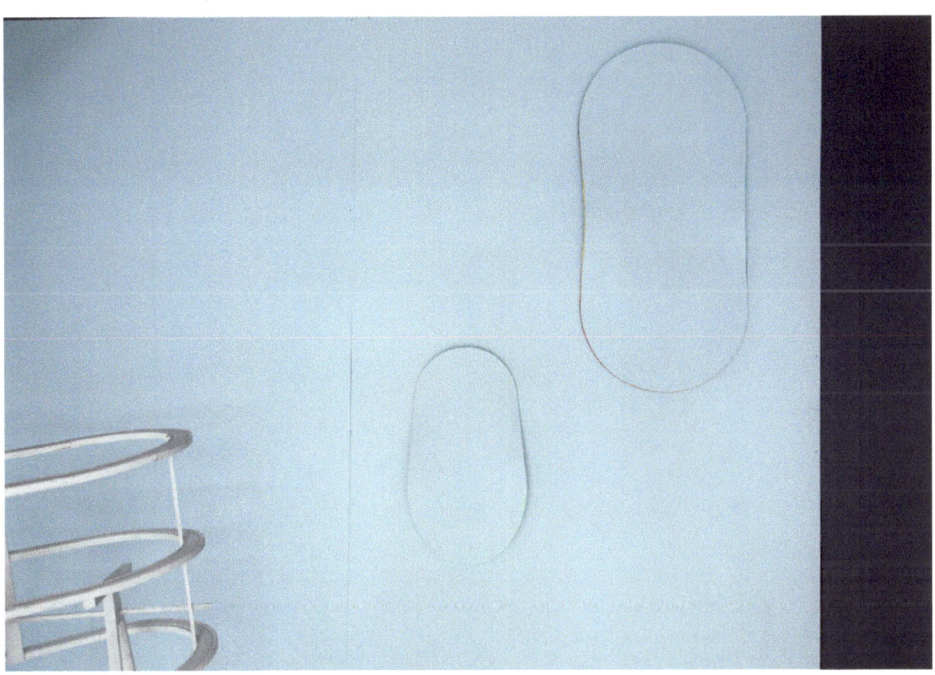

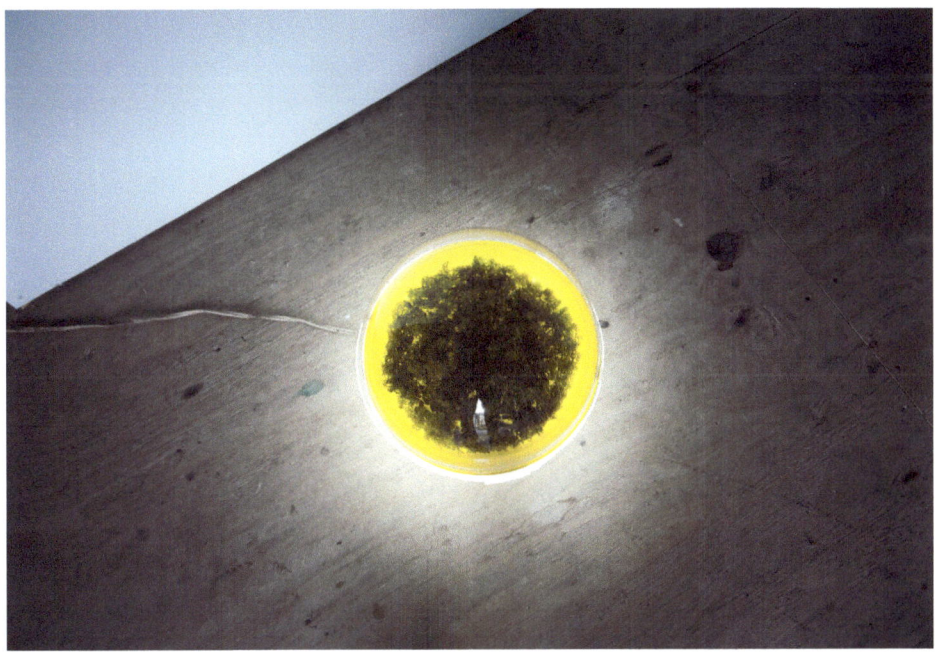

This publication accompanies the exhibition
Gestures of Orbicular Topology, curated by Arthur
Menezes Brum and presented at White Flag,
Brooklyn, NY, June 3, 2010 – June 5, 2011.

First published in the United States of
America in 2011 by Math Practice, LLC.
325 Melrose St. 2L
Brooklyn, NY 11237
www.math-practice.org

White Flag
114 Wilson Ave.
Brooklyn, NY 11221
www.thewhiteflag.org

ISBN 978-0-9836425-1-0

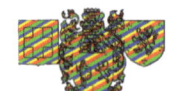

www.ingramcontent.com/pod-product-compliance
Lightning Source LLC
Chambersburg PA
CBHW040825180526
45159CB00001B/67